CALIFORNIA

88 GREAT VACATIONS AND EASY OUTINGS

CALIFORNIA

88 GREAT VACATIONS AND EASY OUTINGS

Lou Bignami

Country Roads Press
Oaks, Pennsylvania

88 Great California Vacations and Easy Outings

Published by Country Roads Press
P.O. Box 838, 2170 West Drive
Oaks, PA 19456

Text design by Allen Crider.

ISBN 1-56626-161-9

Library of Congress Cataloging-in-Publication Data

Bignami, Louis V.
88 great vacations and easy outings : California / Lou Bignami.
p. cm.
Includes index.
ISBN 1-56626-161-9 (alk. paper)
1. California—Guidebooks. 2. Vacations—California—Guidebooks. I. Title.
F859.3.B53 1996
917.9404'53—dc21 96-29486
CIP

Special Sales
Bulk purchases of Country Roads Press guides are available to corporations at special discounts. The Special Sales Department can produce custom editions to be used as premiums and/or for sales promotion to suit individual needs. Existing editions can be produced with custom cover imprints such as corporate logos. For more information write to: Special Sales, Country Roads Press, P.O. Box 838, Oaks, PA 19456.

Printed in Canada.
10 9 8 7 6 5 4 3 2 1

Contents

CENTRAL CALIFORNIA

The Central Coast

Monterey Bay

Inland Action

Fun in the Foothills

The Central Sierra

NORTHERN CALIFORNIA

SOUTHERN CALIFORNIA

L.A. and Environs

1.

Biking, Blading, or Bumming the Beach

Santa Monica Pier may be the most photographed pier in Southern California. It's a nice place to start a bike ride or, for the frisky, a roller-blade run down the beach path to Palos Verdes, at the upscale end of the water. This section's by-passed by Highway 1 so you enjoy less traffic while you sample a series of old-style L.A. beach towns. Most days, you'll find surfers, Frisbee flippers, bird-watchers—avian and human—and the usual assortment of L.A. beach types. You can get a map if you like, but it's hard to get lost with the surf on one side and Highway 1 on the other.

It's probably best to rent a three speed—you don't need ten speeds on the flat and you don't have to wonder if your back seat partner's peddling. Kids' bikes can come with training wheels. Day rates are about twice the two-hour rate, so they make sense and allow you time to stop, fish, swim, or picnic. A group trip with shuttle cars is available, so you need only bike in one direction.

Expect a sense of changing values as you leave Santa Monica State Park and zip under the pier into Venice where old hippies share the sun with hard bodies of either gender. There's street entertainment of surprising variety—dubious to delightful—and a complete assortment of diet busters. Take the time to check out the fishing action at Venice fishing pier before you cut inland around Marina del Rey, which has a definitive collection of what one wag calls "holes in the water into which you pour your money" at the huge yacht harbor along Ballena Creek.

Marina del Rey, home of Mercedes, exotic coffees, and other diversions for the BMW set, isn't a bad spot for a snack, and since you're biking or blading, you won't be tempted by upscale shopping. So it's on to Playa del Rey and the industrial offerings of El Secundo with its oil refineries and the thundering flock of 747s out of LAX. A bit farther south, you can watch hang-gliders soaring off the bluffs and landing on or, in the case of beginners, crashing onto, the beach.

Manhattan Beach, Hermosa Beach, and Redondo Beach flow one into the other. Quiet beach towns with sand-blasted pastel homes jammed shoulder to shoulder in their fight to see the sea move past like an old 1950s' beach movie with Annette Funicello and her pals. It gets progressively quieter as you pedal south toward the massive headlands of Palos Verdes. Then, as Sepulveda Boulevard, a.k.a. Highway 1, turns away from the ocean to follow the Kings Highway toward San Diego, it's time to turn back and run the nineteen miles of the South Bay Bike Trail back to Santa Monica.

For more information:

Bike Trail Coordinator, Country Roads Department, Box 4089, Los Angeles, CA 90051.

For bike and blade rentals: Santa Monica, Venice, Playa del Rey, Hermosa Beach, and Redondo Beach all offer bikes.

Tip: If you have small children and don't shuttle, start in the middle of the route, bike to one end, head back and drop them off to fly kites or eat saltwater candy until you return.

2.
Hollywood and Scenic Downtown Burbank

Four studios to tour, a fleet of bus or van rides past stars' homes, fliers that tell you where movie or TV shows shoot in and around L.A., plus other oddities such as stars' hand and foot prints, names, and five-pointed stars in the street testify to the L.A. basin's importance in the movie business. You'd have to push hard to enjoy everything. Universal Studios Hollywood, in particular, can take a whole day and is the choice if you can only visit one studio. Add a visit to what's now called Mann's Chinese Theater, check out the dubious architectural delights of the Capitol Records Building, and try a visit to the Hollywood Bowl.

To see more, you need to start early and stay late to cover everything. Visit Warner Brothers and NBC one day, check out Paramount and Universal Studios another, and you're on a manageable schedule. Write for free studio-audience tickets to TV shows, too; mention the dates you'd like to visit and include a stamped, self-addressed envelope.

NBC: As I write this, NBC's Burbank Studios host Jay Leno's *Tonight Show.* That seems fair, as his predecessor Johnny Carson never let up on "scenic downtown Burbank." Maybe that's the price you pay in a city named after a botanist. In any case, there's usually a line of locals and visitors waiting to get into the *Tonight Show* audience. However, if you can't get inside that one, you can get a closer look at the set, see other shows filming on the lot that day, and take a quick tour of the wardrobe and production areas.

Paramount Pictures: Paramount Studios' double arched gates with the fancy grilles look like the old Bronson Street Gate that Gloria Swanson drove

Hollywood's Chinese Theater

through in *Sunset Boulevard.* The original gates saw most of the old-time Hollywood stars back in the days when Cecil B. DeMille directed here. Classics such as *Godfather I* and *II*, and *Forrest Gump* were filmed here, as were TV shows such as *Frasier, Wings,* and *Star Trek: Deep Space Nine.* So you've got rather a good chance to see a star on a break on your tour of the sixty-three acres of back-lot that, like Warner Brothers, seems to concentrate the celebrities better than Universal Studios' vast operation.

Universal Studios Hollywood: No question but

that this is the flossiest, as well as the world's largest at four hundred and twenty acres, film complex anywhere. Given the time, plan to spend an entire day here—the average visit is eight hours—with the rides, studio attractions, shows, and simply exploring. If you're rushed, try the forty-five-minute train ride through the back lot. There's far too much to cover but, when your feet die, you can sample one of eighteen(!) different movies in the Odeon Theatres.

If you only have time for a single studio tour, this is definitely the one!

Warner Brothers: Jack Warner built a wonder set of streets for the back lot of his studio. The "New York Street" set was used in forty-eight films from Bogart movies to *Batman*. The "Midwest Street" and the "Western" back lot used in *Bonanza, Little House on the Prairie, and Maverick* should look familiar to any film buff.

If you can, opt for the VIP tour and reserve a spot in the studio dining room for lunch—it's rated the best studio restaurant in the Southland and a great spot to see how little food actors eat.

For more information:

For television tickets, call NBC-TV at 818-840-3438 or try the window at 3000 West Alameda Avenue, Burbank, CA 91523, from 9:00 A.M. to 5:00 P.M. weekdays.

For information at Paramount, call 213-956-5575 or try the window at 860 Gower Street, Hollywood, CA 90038, from 8:00 A.M. to 4:00 P.M. weekdays.

Call Audiences Unlimited at Warner Brothers, 818-506-0043, or write 5726 Sunset Boulevard, Hollywood, CA 90025, 8:30 A.M. to 6 P.M.

Call Universal Studios Hollywood, 818-508-9600, or write, 100 Universal City Plaza, Universal City, CA 91608.

3.
Ethnic L.A.

Los Angeles used to be called "a collection of villages in search of a city." Now that the downtown's sprouted skyscrapers and a "real" business district, this may not quite be true, but L.A. retains its multicultural nature that really started when the Spanish met the local Native Americans. These days, some jest that L.A. has more Hispanics than some Central American countries, and it's clear that Chinatown, Little Tokyo, and Koreatown have joined Olvera Street as ethnic enclaves worth a visit.

A weekend in each area—all have nearby lodgings, restaurants, and shopping that make you think you're in a foreign country—isn't unrealistic. There's so much to do that you'd otherwise have to seek out the best attractions.

Olvera Street and El Pueblo: The forty-four acres of El Pueblo de Los Angeles's historic section aren't as old as you might expect. The oldest building (named after a relative of mine) is the Avila Adobe, built in 1818. It looks reasonably authentic and does have a decent church and a nice fire fighting museum. There's shopping and a chance to stroll. Don't miss nearby Union Station, one of the best old train stations in the West.

However, since we know which sections are safest, we usually head for East L.A.'s local neighborhood restaurants, shopping, and vibrant Hispanic community. Mexicans, Salvadorans , Nicaraguans, and other Latinos seem to get along reasonably well. Safety—at least during daylight hours and with an eye for the feel of the neighborhood—isn't a major problem on main streets. Still, it's sad that there's not a better connection between Hispanic neighborhoods and the old downtown.

Little Tokyo: The New Otami Hotel and its wonderful roof-top gardens are the center of today's Little Tokyo. We treasure the peace and quiet of the James Irvine Sunken Gardens as well. Several Buddhist temples, a lively historic district, and the largest Japanese community in the United States add up to plenty to do, even if you don't check out the Kabuki in the largest cultural center in the United States.

We're particularly fond of the food here. Street stands, sushi bars, and small shops serve bentos or rice and seaweed-wrapped treats, tempura, and wonderful smoked noodles called udon. As is usually the case, check out the smaller shops on side streets where locals eat. A little bit here, a little bit there lets you graze as you go. Hot green tea is surpassingly cooling on hot days.

Seasonal festivals such as the Chinese New Year offer all sorts of attractions; but we find that the less-crowded weekends present top value, and as always, extended weekends or midweek trips let you savor the neighborhood with minimal tourists.

Koreatown: Koreatown and the Vietnamese enclaves toward Chinatown offer something a bit different, even for an old Asian hand. Korean art, pottery in particular, deserves a look.

Chinatown: Chinatown lurks just south of Dodger Stadium—do check the hill behind the stadium for its old Victorian homes, dandy b and bs, and other attractions that make it a popular spot with film makers—where its Massive East Gate beckons tourists. Take a look at Sun Yat Sen's statue; he wrote the Chinese Constitution while hiding out in, of all places, Marysville, California.

Clothing (tailors with and without Hong Kong

branches are wonderful), food, and crafts suit savvy shoppers. As usual in Asian areas, things aren't always what they seem. Shops around Bamboo or Mandarin Plaza get much of the tourist traffic, while smaller shops can hide wonderful Chinese antiques, and dim sup or wonton noodles from a storefront cafe may be better than those you find in more upscale surroundings. Dim sum, where you can simply point at treats as they pass on carts and pay by the number of plates that accumulate on your table, is best sampled with a group.

Tip: Check out the wonderful sweet rolls at the Phoenix Bakery and, if you can, scan the nontourist side of Chinese menus as many restaurants have special dishes that never make the English side of the menu. While most restaurants are still Cantonese, you'll do well to explore other options. Go with a group and order as the Chinese do, so you each share a dish plus have one more for the table.

4.

Pier Pleasures

California visitors who don't walk, fish, or rubberneck the Golden State's hundreds of piers miss out on some of the best birding, scenery, and, perhaps most interesting, people-watching in America. As the old saw goes, "they shook America and the nuts rolled west." I'm prejudiced, as I grew up fishing Berkeley Pier back in its salad days before the yuppie invasion. I caught halibut off Santa Cruz piers and, when we visited relatives in Los Angeles, could take the bus and spend a day in the fresh ocean air.

Los Angeles piers offer incredible variety. My own favorite's Malibu Pier. Where else could you see Bruce Willis catching perch or use your binoculars to check out the star-studded action on the beach? This is a decent spot to fish, too, with a solid basement of smaller fish such as perch and summer mackerel and a sprinkling of halibut as well as a toothsome selection of sharks. You can, as is the case with most L.A. piers, rent tackle, but, as is also generally true, you're better off buying lunch or its makings at a shop on shore.

Santa Monica Municipal Pier, right in the shop-until-you-drop beach zone, is perhaps more popular with walkers than with anglers as the sand bottom restricts the catch to perch and such. Then too, when the surf's up, the fishing's down. So you're better off moving on to an in-bay pier or to freshwater. For added enjoyment, there are always string bikinis or even a ride on the fenced-in merry-go-round that's been in more movies than Bob Hope.

Redondo Beach Pier may offer the best fishing along the L.A. coast during summer when the bonito run to hit anchovies and lures. Otherwise, you're left with a decent restaurant and limited bait and tackle. During the rest of the year, the fishery for sharks and rays is the choice for those who fish big bait on the bottom with heavy gear.

Manhattan Beach Municipal Pier's the new kid on the piscatorial block. It went up in 1992, and the fishing's a lot like that on Redondo Beach, except there are more mackerel and fewer bonito. The bait shop's okay, but you need to cross over the frontage road for decent food and such.

Hermosa Beach Municipal Pier seems easy to overlook. The results here are best in summer, especially for mackerel. There's always the chance of a halibut or ray, and the atmosphere seems quieter and more laid back than at other piers.

Gearing Up: Any kind of freshwater spinning or casting gear works. Fly rods are marginal unless you can steeple or roll cast. Try ten- to fifteen-pound test lines, size six hooks baited with pile worms or anchovies, and fish on the bottom with a weight or under the bobber when mackerel or bonito run. A crab net or pier gaff is handy so you need not walk big fish into the beach, but other anglers usually offer theirs as well as needed help.

Do bring a jacket, as it can get breezy. Don't forget a bird book. Shore and ocean birds deserve identification.

For more information:

For general fishing reports, try the *Los Angeles Times*. If you're on the Internet, check Lou Bignami's Fine Fishing on the World Wide Web at finefishing.com for daily pier reports and weekly baja and freshwater results.

Malibu Pier, 310-456-8030.

Manhattan Beach Parks and Recreation, 310-545-5621.

5.

Rides, Motion Sickness, and Other Kids' Stuff

Back in salad days when we visited friends in Pasadena, my mother would dump me off at the La Brea tar pits where I'd spend a happy day checking out the fossils and bugging the curators before being picked up at closing time. This, and fishing off Santa Monica Pier, were my two favorite L.A. activities, so I probably have a perverted idea of what kids like. I do know I hate theme parks. With input from an assortment of ten small fry, here are their ten favorite places in order of preference.

Time allowances are approximate to help you plan your weekend. Do remember that many rides have height and other requirements for kids.

Disneyland: This is the most popular destination in the L.A. basin if you don't mind lines. (Or schedule a visit midweek during the fall or winter.) Tip: Get there when it opens and try the rides farthest from the entrance first and work your way back. Don't eat lunch or dinner since lines are shortest then. Teenagers may be too blasé for this one as the rides, except possibly for Space Mountain if you get car sick, are rather on the tame side. (Allow eight hours.)

Raging Waters: If Raging Waters weren't open only from May through October, the kids we interviewed would be terminally water-logged. Big kids adore the speed slides and the chutes on the forty-four acres. There's a kids' play area and pool for the small or timid, but the adventurous aquatic child will have to be hauled away from this one. I rather liked the rides myself, even though one kid called me "the whale."

"Okay, if I have to wait an hour after lunch before I ride the chutes, I won't eat lunch." (Allow eight hours.)

Six Flags Magic Mountain: "Killer coaster" remarks suggest adults might want to eat lightly before they try "Batman, the Ride" and the other infamous diet aids here. Kids who train here probably end up in the Blue Angels. There's no other place in Southern California that matches its rides. While small fry like the petting zoo, "ten years old and up" seems a good rule for the rest of the activities. (Take smaller kids to the L.A. Children's Museum, instead.) Take a Dramamine if you run to motion sickness.

Not for parents who don't want to watch their

kids flying about upside down with their hands over their heads. (Allow eight hours.)

Knott's Berry Farm: "Slingshot," "Slammer," and a batch of other rides keep the teens dashing for shorter lines than we found at Disneyland. Small fry adore "Camp Snoopy." I like their fried chicken and find the atmosphere a bit less plastic than most theme parks. It's a nice choice for all ages and a personal favorite. (Allow eight hours.)

Travel Town and Live Steamers: These two railroad attractions are a sneaker for most L.A. visitors. Travel Town is a wonderful transportation museum with steam locomotives kids can climb on and ride—only Sacramento's is a better train museum in California—and the nearby Live Steamers has the largest collection of miniature trains anywhere. It's a decent half day and fits in with a visit to nearby Griffith Observatory or the L.A. Zoo. (Allow three hours.)

Universal Studios Hollywood: We've covered this from the movie/TV viewpoint. As far as rides go, "Back From the Future—The Ride" was "except for the lines, neat!" Kids under ten preferred "Fievel's Playland." I personally appreciated a chance to sit down to watch the Flintstones rock 'n' roll, although I'm not a fan of the music. (Allow eight hours.)

George C. Page Museum of La Brea Discoveries: Aside from complaints about the lack of dinosaurs—the "pits" are Pleistocene and run to saber-toothed cats and such—this was a hit. The museum's a grand improvement over the old university exhibit halls, and the sculpture in the pits show how animals strayed and stuck here. (Note: One very small girl cried about that.) The museum shop's particularly worthwhile. If the small fry insist on dinosaurs, try the Natural History Museum. (Allow two hours.)

Museum of Flying: As is the case with San Diego, wonderful weather made Los Angeles a center of early aviation. Interaction's the name of the game at this fine Santa Monica Airport attraction that's a good stop before a day at the beach. Kids can fiddle, climb in and out, and try design and gear. Now if you want something really aeronautic, check AIR COMBAT U.S.A. for dogfighting at 800-522-7590. (Allow two hours.)

The Beach: Okay, it's not a museum, but all the kids interviewed added, "and we go to the beach, too." Try Venice for a classic collection of "unusual" folks.

Check out the Santa Monica Pier merry-go-round as an add-on to a Museum of Flying visit or hit one of the local kite shops or bike rental stands. The farther you live from the ocean, the bigger the impression the beach makes. (Allow eight hours.)

Gene Autry Western Heritage Museum and the L.A. Zoo: Two of our sample kids are Indian buffs and mentioned the costumes at the museum, but the hands-on kids' exhibits eat up a couple of hours. None of the kids know who Gene Autry was. Too bad. Gene Autry turned B-run Western movies and singing into a fortune that bought a chain of radio and TV stations and the baseball club.

The L.A. Zoo next door isn't a bad choice if you can't see the San Diego Zoo on a given trip. L.A.'s got nifty koalas and a wonderful primate collection. Did you know zoo animals sulk when the zoo's closed? Given L.A.'s colorful inhabitants, visitors can be as entertaining as displays. There's a dandy shop and several good spots to eat as you watch the passing parade. A good winter, fall, or spring choice.

For more information:

L.A. Parks and Recreation Department, 213-485-5555.

6.

Southern California Snow

Southern California skiers do not have to zoom up Highway 395 to Mammoth Mountain, the largest ski resort with the longest season in the Sierras. They can find quality cross-country and downhill skiing just an hour from Highway 2 in the Angeles National Forest, or they can drive a bit longer to Big Bear or even combine some summer sun in Palm Springs with nordic skiing at the top of the Aerial Tramway. Choice! That's the recipe for fun in the snow for those who may focus more on fun in the sun!

New skiers should consider day trips with lessons at cross-country resorts that have set tracks for those going out for the first time so they can learn basics, such as falling, where injury is less likely. Beginners might start at smaller, less expensive resorts that suit family skiers—kids do stray at big resorts! Minimum gear includes warm gloves, sweaters, hats, and wool socks. Water- resistant clothing helps beginners who fall stay dry. Sunglasses and sunscreen protect against sunburn in the bright, harsh sun. Tote a change of clothing for the trip home and, for those on tight budgets, full brown-bags that let the ravenous skip $2 hot dogs on the slopes. Apply these tips on a sunny day and enjoy a quality introduction or return to the snow on Southern California's ten best ski resorts.

Skiers who brave the Angeles Crest Highway find a variety of cross-country resorts around the Newcom Ranch Inn and decent downhill skiing at Mountain High East, Mountain High West, and family resorts Mountain Waterman, Kratka Ridge, and Ski Sunrise.

Mountain Highs make a lot of snow. Beginners do very well in the beginners' bowl and getting off chairs one, two, and three. A mile-and-a-half run challenges fitter skiers. Night skiing opens up these areas during the week, and kids under ten ski free with an adult. The Children's Buckaroo program, a special for three to seven year olds, lets parents ski on their own. Both resorts offer full services, so they seem a good place for beginners and intermediates to ski while experts crash and burn at Ski Sunrise just up the road.

Ski Sunrise has a special Scorpion Ski beginner package for easy starts off Poma A and Rope Two B. That makes up for very steep expert runs off Giant Poma D. Tickets are limited, so crowds are controlled even on big holiday weekends. This may be the only ski resort in California where you park on top and ski down to the lifts!

Mountain Waterman is a family-type day-use ski hill where two children under twelve can ski free with one adult. More than half of the runs are advanced, but beginners find good snow and easy runs near the bottom of chair Number 1. Kratka Ridge is even smaller, with short runs and a lively beginners' area near the rope tows and near Number 2 double chair when they have snow.

Big Bear Resorts, off Highway 18 via the Lucerne Valley, offer a variety of choices. Snow Valley is a major area with extensive snow-making. Ski until 9:00 P.M. Wednesday through Sunday. By segregating advanced skiers to their own side of the mountain, this fine resort makes life easier for beginners and intermediates.

Snow Summit covers ninety-five percent of its mountain with artificial snow and gets skiers onto it with ten chair lifts. With seventy-five percent of the mountain rated for beginners and intermediates and a limited sale of lift tickets, it's no surprise that reservations are suggested on weekends and holidays.

Goldmine snow-making covers a hundred percent of its slopes off Geronimo Peak with two race hills, a special kids' program, Minor's Camp, and a number of special day activities between Thanksgiving and Easter. Ask about group and other special rates.

Snow Forest offers inexpensive family skiing with a nice beginner area near parking on Siberia Mountain.

Odd and unusual add-ons include the following:

Las Vegas visitors who need a break from the tables might consider Lee Canyon, an hour from town at a 9,500-foot elevation, where complete snow- making and a nice snow/play area and nordic skiing contribute to the quiet setting.

Skiing in Palm Springs? Almost! A decent nordic ski area rents cross-country skis and snowshoes at an 8,515-foot elevation at the top of the Aerial Tram. This is slog-and-sweat trail skiing, not set tracks, but worth the effort for experienced cross-country skiers in search of something different.

Something different! That's a good description of Southern California skiing. Each resort offers a unique experience, each suits a different skier. It may take a winter to find the resort that suits you best, but that's the challenge of Southern California snow.

For more information and reservations:

(Always call for road and snow information before you leave home.)

Goldmine Ski Area, Box 6812, Big Bear Lake, CA 92315, 714-585-2519.

Kratka Ridge Ski Area, Star Route, La Canada, CA 91011, 818-449-1749.

Lee Canyon, Ski Lee, 1552 Winwood Street, Las Vegas, NV 89108, 702-872-5462.

Mountain High East/West, Mountain High Ski Area, Box 993, Wrightwood, CA 92397, 213-460-6911.
Snow Forest, Box 1711, Big Bear, CA 92314, 714-866-8891.
Snow Summit, Big Bear Lake, CA 92315, 714-866-5766.
Snow Valley, Box 8, Running Springs, CA 92382, 714-867-2751.

7.
Weekend with a Queen

With Howard Hughes's *Spruce Goose* gone north to Oregon, the *Queen Mary* and its associated shops and other diversions offer more than enough attraction for anyone to spend a weekend with a queen. The glorious old vessel is now a tourist attraction, a decent restaurant, and perhaps the largest Art Deco object ever built.

The R.M.S. (Royal Mail Ship) *Queen Mary* was commissioned back in 1925 and launched on her maiden voyage to New York in 1938. She saw yeoman service during WWII when she safely carried about eight hundred thousand soldiers during six years of wartime service and managed a thousand and one trans-Atlantic crossings—her fastest was three days, twenty-one hours, and forty-eight minutes.

However, it was clear by the end of WWII that due to aviation advances usual in wartime, the grand liners were endangered. Jet transports finished them off. So the city of Long Beach sprang for $3.5 million to acquire it, and various management groups have spent many more millions since.

The result's a classic attraction with the largest

cabins ever built for a ship that sported exotic—at that time—Formica and plastic bathroom fixtures. Public areas include the three-story-tall dining room, where you can enjoy a special Sunday brunch or the interesting children's playhouse or first-class drawing rooms.

Visitors can check out the original staterooms, crew's quarters, gym, or the engine room and wheelhouse displays that re-enact a near collision at sea. Add a huge ship's propeller, anchor, and other items, and you've spent an enjoyable hour or two.

Worth the extra cost is the Captain's Tour that explores areas such as the first-class swimming pool, salons, and the spaces where the ship's twenty-seven boilers once stood. Probably not worth the cost are the doodads sold in the shopping village just outside the entrance to the ship, but that's a matter of taste.

While day trips are possible, and the Sunday brunch is particularly recommended, you also can enjoy a Saturday stay in the larger-than-usual staterooms of the Queen Mary Hotel aboard the liner. Dinner in the elegant restaurant isn't outstanding when compared to the old days, but the 1930s' Art Deco lounge offers a wonderful view of the Pacific Ocean.

Then, too, there's a special feeling about the ship that carried passengers such as Winston Churchill, the Duke of Windsor, Greta Garbo, Fred Astaire, and most of the other rich and famous just after WWII. A walk on the deck, sitting in a deck chair, or coming back to your cabin with its turned-down bed put you in touch with times past. Faster, at least with travel, isn't always better!

For more information:

***Queen Mary*, Box 8, Long Beach, CA 90801, 310-435-3511.**

8.
Wild Wheels

I adore long drives and old cars, new cars, hot cars, or cool cars, for you can take the kid out of California, but you can't take California out of this overage, overweight kid. Like most California natives, my love of automobiles runs me past museums, racetracks, and anywhere else that has a smog-producing vehicle.

California, especially Southern California, has a car culture—Chicanos with their low riders, old-car buffs with anything at least twenty years old, and, for the young of all ages, rag tops that testify to the virtues of open air and improving smog conditions in the L.A. basin. Practically speaking, the average Southern Californian commutes between an hour and two hours each way. Note: The time you hear is the speaker's best time ever and not to be believed.

Driving on L.A. freeways, especially if you live in a happy place where traffic jams mean you miss two light changes, can be brutal during what locals call "commute" hours. As near as I can tell, these run from 6:00 in the morning until 11:00 A.M. and from 3:00 to 7:00 P.M. In between, you've the lunch rush and, in the evening until about 3:00 A.M., the charge of the chemically enhanced. So, as much as I like to drive, I stay off the freeways.

One good way to do this is the alpine route out of San Bernadino—a hundred and one miles of Rim of the World Drive that runs up Highway 30 to Big Bear Lake at elevations between 5000 and 7200 feet. Side roads to spots such as Big Pine Flats and the Holcomb Valley put you into little-known gold-mining country and run you through some of the nicest cedar, piñon, ponderosa, and jeffrey pine anywhere.

The area looks more like Lake Tahoe than Southern California and offers a wonderful break from summer smog. The old town of Belleville and the unique *assistencia*, or branch mission, at San Antonio de Pala deserve a look. The latter is a branch of Mission San Luis Rey over in Oceanside and is still an active parish church for the local Pauma Indians.

Closer to L.A., try the fifty miles of the Mullholland Scenic Corridor that runs through the Santa Monica Mountains to Leo Carrillo. About half of all low-budget "drive-until-you-die" and tacky monster movies are filmed here, and the views are superb for a day or two after a rain. Spring's the best season for green hills.

Rather more upscale is the short fifteen-mile Palos Verdes Scenic Drive. It connects with a bike trail described in Chapter 1: Biking, Blading, and Bumming the Beach. Richard Dana's classic book *Two Years Before the Mast* offers the best look at early sailing days in Hispanic California. These days, the Palos Verdes runs to the good life.

Urban drives along Sunset or Supulveda, from the end of one to the end of the other, offer an interesting cross section of L.A. However, the best urban drive in the south is the twenty-five mile San Diego Scenic Drive. It ranks with San Francisco's 49 Mile Drive if you run it on a weekend to avoid traffic. Expect to take an hour for a quick look, then allow the rest of the weekend to go back and see everything (see Chapters 9, 10 and 11 on San Diego).

Another dandy, and much more bucolic, drive is the twenty-one miles of Erosion Road near Anza Borrego Desert State Park. This is out of San Diego in the dry and dusty desert that's best visited after spring rains.

Roads with bends, two-way traffic, scenic turnouts, historical stops, old-time local malt shops, and a sense of California's pre-freeway past repay time spent with indelible memories.

All of these are delicious on a nice day when the traffic's good, the air's clear, and the music, and your companion, suit your taste.

All routes are better if you drive something other than the boring econo-box most of us rent.

One way to do this is with something from Budget's Beverly Hills Car Collection, found in those two centers of economic excess, Marina del Rey and Beverly Hills. The Rolls Royce is busted as I write this, but you can find BMWs, Mercedes, Ferraris, and other hot iron at prices in the "if-you-have-to-ask, you-can't-afford-it" class. Well, figure $250 to $400 a day plus half a buck a mile. Of course, there's a complimentary pickup at LAX through Marina del Rey.

AutoExotica adds Lamborghinis, Maseratis, and Excaliburs and even has a one-way rental from L.A. to San Francisco. Stops at the Madona Inn in San Luis Obispo are optional. If you'd prefer to leave the driving to someone else, L.A. has more limos, luxury motor coaches, and other exotic wheels available than anywhere else I know. Just don't try for a rental on Oscar night!

For more information:
AutoExotica, 213-652-2834.
Budget's Beverly Hills Car Collection, 800-227-2117.

San Diego

9.

Balboa Park—Best in the West

When Balboa "discovered" the Pacific Ocean for Spain, he certainly never envisioned a namesake park, let alone such a wonderful example of urban design—for San Diego's Balboa Park could be the best urban park in the world. For one, its San Diego Zoo tops zoo experts' lists. Plus, the park's incredible selection of museums, exhibits, theaters, and cultural activities attracts hordes of locals and foreign visitors. Darwinian "survival of the fittest" enters in here, too. With so many outdoor options available year-round in balmy weather, the park must offer something special to lure locals and visitors from beach and bay.

My wife and I visit San Diego often, but we never have time to see everything in Balboa Park. So we separate to see our favorites. I gawk at automobiles, aircraft, and zoo birds. My wife checks out koalas, crafts at the Spanish Village, and the Timken Art Gallery. We meet for lunch in the fourteenth-century Moorish-palace atmosphere of the Cafe del Rey Moro. Then we share the San Diego Museum of Art and Art Institute shows.

Even without special seasonal attractions, you could take a week to see everything. Your tastes doubtless differ from ours, too. Therefore, we offer a short rundown on each activity class so you can route your visit to suit the time you have to invest.

Flora and Fauna: While life "is a beach" on the coast, in Balboa Park it is exhibitions of fauna and flora centered in the San Diego Zoo. First-time visitors should consider a double-decker bus orientation tour or try the Skyfari for an overview. After obligatory visits to the koalas and pygmy chimps and a look at the scheduled pandas, you can return to the exhibits that tempt you most.

For example, the wonderful birds or rare "hand-painted" Mhorr gazelles. I like to walk and look, then sit and watch to rest the feet. Kids have their special zoo, too. If you tire, take the small fry to the Butterfly Rides, classic carousel, or miniature Super Chief train ride by the zoo entrance. You might try the pedicabs from the zoo to the far end of the lot or opt for a carriage ride as well if you arrive late and spaces near the zoo entrance are filled.

With so many animal exhibits, it's difficult, but worthwhile, to save time for the flora. Some zoo trees and many park plants are outstanding examples of their species. Garden buffs enjoy the Alcazar Garden, Lily Pond, and the Cactus and Zoro Gardens. There is a memorial rose garden as well. Check park maps carefully to find other attractions.

If it rains, consider the Natural History Museum. It is extremely strong on local and Southwestern ecology. The hands-on video learning center and weekend nature walks and films can save a washed-out day when you can't visit the zoo.

Arts and Crafts: Museums easily fill rainy days. Given the spectacular scenery and, until the recent population explosion of smog-makers, the clear air, strong support for San Diego art museums should be no surprise. Since my wife and I are professional photographers, we first visit the Museum of Photographic Arts when major exhibitions grace the walls. The usual mix of lectures, workshops, and films more than repay the admission. On weekends, afternoon group tours offer a bonus.

The Timken Art Gallery is the "best of show" for Balboa Park's art offerings. It's small, but the paintings by masters such as Breugel and Rembrandt are outstanding. If you don't favor gilt, skip the Russian icons and head for the San Diego Museum of Art's larger, if more eclectic, collections. Italian Renaissance and Spanish Baroque, the strong points of the collection, aren't my cup of tea, so I check the Asian art and French Impressionists before it's tea time at the Sculpture Garden Cafe.

There is still more art. The San Diego Art Institute features the work of local artists of varied merit and, now and then, professional shows. We find more lively artists, and skilled artisans, at the Spanish Village Arts and Crafts Center. At various times, we've watched potters and stained-glass experts here. It is the spot for an afternoon break.

Science and Technology: The *Spirit of St. Louis* was built in San Diego, and a replica hangs in the AeroSpace Historical Center, one of several park museums that reflect the importance of science and technology in San Diego. The San Diego Aerospace Museum holds a dandy collection of historical aircraft and warbirds such as Spitfires and a Mig-15. The Aerospace Hall of Fame is part of the package. It's a bargain if you can keep aviation buffs out of the gift shop!

You get into the Reuben H. Fleet Space Theater and Science Center on the same ticket. If you can, hit the first show at 9:45 A.M. before crowds gather. The dome-shaped screen and hundred and fifty-two speakers redefine "surrounded by sound." If you don't arrive early and miss the cut for seats, you can easily spend time between shows in the hands-on exhibits. Don't bring teenagers here in the morning. You may not get them away from the aircraft exhibits!!

A few hundred yards away, the San Diego Automotive Museum delights Ford and other automobile buffs. Local Ford dealers contributed $150,000, so there are lots of Fords on hand! Other interesting vehicles include early examples of RVs. Warning: Auto buffs should not browse the library. Comprehensive collections of repair manuals and the complete collection of the Horseless Carriage Foundation's books would take months to cover. The museum is a fine value at $3.50.

Trains, even models, always get my attention. The San Diego Model Railroad Museum has twenty-one thousand square feet of O, HO, and N scale model railways that replicate San Diego and nearby tracks. Children find the twenty-two-foot-tall railroad semaphore outside the museum a wonder even before it moves—its gears turn, flags wave, and lights flash. This is well worth the five-minute wait.

History and Culture: San Diego certainly reflects its long, multicultural heritage in its other museums. Centro Cultural de la Raza runs to colorful Mexican, Indian, and Chicano exhibits. The murals are worth a look. The House of Pacific Relations huddles in a collection of small cottages, each reflecting a different nation. On Sunday afternoons, all sorts of ethnic diversions—bagpipes and dim sum, for example—vary in quality and taste. They, like the nearby United Nations Building and shop, are worth a look if you are in the area with time to spare.

The Museum of San Diego History and San Diego Hall of Champions suit locals interested in the minutiae of the area's history. Try the San Diego Museum of Man instead. Baskets, pottery, and jewelry rank with the best art in town. Weaving and tortilla-making exhibits are first-rate. So is the gift shop, with some of the best values in the park.

Fuel Stops: Second to a good pair of walking shoes, food to fuel your wanderings is a prime need. Food in the park and at the zoo varies. Creative Croissants, in the Aerospace buildings, get full marks for light lunches. The Sculpture Garden Cafe has lighter items (my wife calls these "ladies' lunches"). The Chocolate Lily Express Cafe runs to Italian coffee-house specialties.

The Cafe del Rey Moro décor seems more delightful than the food, but they do sell decent box lunches. We haven't tried dinner with the epicurean delights of San Diego just outside the park. Pizza and hot dogs at concession stands and the food at the zoo did not impress us on our last visit. A trip to a local deli and brown-bagging seem a fine choice on any budget!

Balboa Park isn't limited to culture buffs. Families spread picnics under the trees. Soccer, rugby, and baseball games ebb and flow. Hikers, joggers, bikers, and runners whip along park paths. More sedentary visitors fly kites and model airplanes. Balboa Park greets a variety of visitors and refreshes their recollection of art and the outdoors. It's the best in the West. Perhaps it's the best downtown park anywhere!

For more information:
(San Diego area code is 619)
AeroSpace Historical Center, 234-8291.
Centro Cultural de la Raza, 235-6135.
House of Pacific Relations, 466-7654.
Museum of Photographic Arts, 239-5262.
Museum of San Diego History, 232-6203.
Natural History Museum, 232-3821.
Reuben H. Fleet Space Theater and Science Center, 238-1233.
San Diego Art Institute, 234-5946.
San Diego Automotive Museum, 231-2886.

San Diego Hall of Champions, 234-2544.
San Diego Model Railroad Museum, 437-4316.
San Diego Museum of Art, 232-7931.
San Diego Zoo, 234-3154.
Spanish Village Arts and Crafts Center, 235-6809.
Timken Art Gallery, 239-5548.
United Nations Building, 233-8457.

10.

San Diego Wet

Look across San Diego Bay at Coronado, where "old admirals who don't play golf well enough to live in Carmel rust out their retirement years," and you'll see a host of Navy craft from carriers on down to gigs. Coronado's also the home base for Navy Seals, the hard cases some call "wet Green Berets"—but not to their faces. Visit their training area if you want to see disgustingly fit folks staying that way on surf and sand.

Just about any kind of craft that floats calls San Diego Bay home. Even the *Love Boats* head out of San Diego part of the year on their trips to Puerto Vallarta, Mazatlan, and Cabo San Lucas. Expect to see sternwheelers, all sorts of sailboats, and the *Princess of the Waves* hydrofoil, or try a walk around on cruise ships.

The sailing cruise on the *California,* which leaves from the Sheraton Harbor Hotel, offers a good look at the harbor and lets you ease along in typical "rag-bagger" style. Power buffs that the rag-bag set calls "stink-potters" can try the Harbor Excursion Company cruises (their one-hour cruise suits us better than the two-hour journey). Save film for the seals and sea lions that laze on the harbor buoys—these are the only lazy seals you'll see.

On the mainland-side waterfront near the bay

cruise boats, you'll find a flotilla of tuna boats and the always-popular harbor ferry boats that we save for a sit-down cruise at the end of what always seems a tiring San Diego day. These are only a start on the options that can leave you groggy after a nautical weekend.

Nearby, the historic ships of the San Diego Maritime Museum shouldn't be missed. The *Star of India*, a barkentine, and the *Berkeley*, an old San Francisco Bay ferry, offer good value for time spent. You also often can find a Navy vessel that's on active duty, moored, and open for visitors in San Diego. On Armed Forces Day in May, City Week in August, and the Navy's birthday in October, a flotilla of Navy ships opens up for visitors.

All these aquatic options include what's one of the most active "head" or party-boat fishing fleets in North America. You can opt for half-day morning, afternoon, or evening trips to sample the bottom fishing and other action just off the coast. On good days, these trips take yellowtail, skipjack, and even albacore. The rest of the time you'll find a variety of bottom fish and oddments such as mackerel.

Longer trips that start with all-day voyages to provide better fishing and extend out to nearly two weeks offer much better action at a considerable investment in time, equipment, and money. It's wise to sample the short trips first—seasickness for three or four hours is a diet aid, but seasickness, or boredom, for a week or so isn't exactly what most folks have in mind as recreation.

This isn't the reason we pass on dinner cruises on sail and power craft in San Diego Bay. It's because the scenery on trips we've taken seems better than the food. Separate harbor tours and your dining/drinking/dancing costs, which are less, in our opinion, make for better meals.

11.

San Diego Theater, Music, and Night Life

Theater and music can treat your ears, and rest your feet, after a long Balboa Park day. The Old Globe Theatre deserves its Tony Award. Three separate stages, the you-can-hear-a-pin-drop Old Globe, the small Cassius Carter Centre Stage, and the outdoor, and usually balmy, Lowell Davies Festival Theater mix Shakespeare and classics with more modern works. Shakespeare in the Old Globe offers a taste of England.

Since most performances are in the evenings, a visit to the Old Globe won't clog your schedule. My wife notes, "Bundling under a blanket at the Lowell Davies Theatre suits romantics." Last trip, we enjoyed John Goodman of *Rosanne* fame, as Falstaff in a unique joining of both parts of *Henry IV*. He was decent, but outclassed by the Shakespearean specialists. It probably takes time to get used to the odd airliner overhead and the still odder seal chatter from the zoo toward dusk (seals apparently get fed late in the day).

The Starlight Bowl runs summer musicals at 8:00 P.M. from June through September. With 4,324 seats, you might need binoculars if you do not book up front. You miss some theater nuances in the spectacular open-air setting. Generally frisky casts that, with only ten performances per play, have not lost their verve offer good value. Last year, prices were in the $10 to $20 range with copious free parking. Tip: Come early, but park near the lot exits, not the bowl, for a quick getaway.

Children enjoy two special offerings. The Marie Hitchcock Puppet Theater in Balboa Park offers weekly weekend shows of hand, rod, and marionette puppets. The San Diego Guild of Puppetry is one of the best in the world, and it's cheap! Just $1 for kids; $1.50 for adults. The San Diego Junior Theater offers five stage shows in the Casa del Prado Theatre as part of its year-round learning and performance program for eight- to-eighteen-year-old youths. Lots of verve here and not as many fluffed lines as you might expect. A must for families with budding thespians!

Everyone enjoys monster pipe organs, and they don't come any bigger outdoors than in the Spreckles Organ Pavilion. If you schedule your lunch break at 2:00 P.M. on Sundays, you can listen to spectacular organ performances. Some are almost as ornately embellished as the Pavilion.

This by no means exhausts your options. Last visit, there were two touring musicals, drama at the famed La Jolla Playhouse, and a host of lively beach and street entertainers. Add the excellent jazz and entertainment in a host of clubs in Old Town. We also enjoyed a wonderful jazz pianist at the Harbor Sheraton and, the next morning, a classical trio for brunch. Just down the walking paths along the water, we found a New Orleans combo. Farther on (and nothing beats a walk along the water on a balmy evening—that's most of them in San Diego) we ended up with a folk-music group before we returned to the hotel and a final drink in the lounge. Unfortunately, there's so much to do during the day that it's difficult to save energy for the nightlife.

For more information:
(San Diego Area Code is 619)
Old Globe Theatre, 239-2255.
San Diego Junior Theater, 239-1311.
Starlight Bowl, 544-7800.
Marie Hitchcock Puppet Theater in Balboa Park, 466-7128.

12.

Romance at the Del

Back in 1920 when Edward, Prince of Wales, visited San Diego, there was a reception for more than a thousand guests at Coronado's classic Hotel del Coronado. Local folklore insists that one couple, Lieutenant Commander Earl Winfield Spencer Jr. and his wife, Wallis Warfield Spencer, apparently made an impression on the prince—or at least Mrs. Spencer apparently did. Prince Edward, later King, gave up his throne for her in 1936. Hanky-panky isn't anything new. Neither are famous guests like Marilyn Monroe, who stayed here in a cottage on the beach in 1958 during the filming of *Some Like it Hot*. Eleven presidents stayed in the Del and it's one of the most popular honeymoon spots in Southern California.

Today, the Del seems the hot spot for Sunday brunch for San Diego residents, classic-car-club rally types, or savvy visitors. However, you only get the full flavor of the Del when you stay overnight, wander the halls, or explore the grounds preferably hand-in-hand.

It's one of the best classic hotels in the world. You can't fault the site, with the bay on one side and the Pacific and its wide sand beaches beyond. You can't fault the look: The white spun-sugar buildings with their unique peaked red roofs are beautifully apparent all over. You can't fault the hotel's history, the first guests having visited in 1888. How old is that in real terms? The Del was the first hotel in the West to have electricity, and Thomas Alva Edison inspected the job.

As a romantic and relaxing weekend getaway, the Del ranks with the best in the world (I've a

Coronado's Hotel del Coronado

theory that honeymoons are wasted on newlyweds, but that's another story). There's more than enough tension, stress, and exercise just down the beach where the Navy Seals train. So when my wife and I visit, we rarely leave the premises, the pool, the grounds, or the restaurants.

Public rooms, such as the Crown Room with its thirty-three-foot-high ceiling and seating for six hundred, offer something special too. In this case, it's wondering about the thousands of wooden pegs—no nails—that apparently hold up the ceiling. Hanging out in the ornate lobby with its open bird-cage elevator and palms offers world-class people-watching. And a host of dining rooms offer better-than-average food for hotels. We run to fish dishes and the raspberry duck, but the Sunday brunch in the Crown Room is worth reserving early. Do ask about window tables.

We haven't—at least so far—ever stayed in two rooms that were the same size, shape, or décor. According to the Del's manager, no two rooms are alike as the entire hotel was built by relatively untrained Chinese carpenters who learned carpentry, and English, on the job. So the back of the hotel on the west side runs to basic box designs, and the front which they finished after on-the-job training features complex round turrets and wildly attractive arches. At last count, I found seventeen different door sizes and some very unusual wood-working details like pegged panels. Tip: Book in the main-building complex, not the new buildings.

Some rooms feature round parlors, others have private staircases, many have huge bathrooms, and oceanfront rooms in high demand may have lanais. Considering the robes and wonderful room service, each visit's a coddled adventure. It's also a threat to your waistline. Good thing there's a spa, big pool, tennis courts, and other options to work off brunch or dinner.

Of course, if you insist on leaving the palm-studded grounds, you can walk down into Coronado to share upscale shopping with retired admirals and tourists.

For more information:

Hotel Del Coronado, 1500 Orange Avenue, Coronado, CA 92118, 619-522-8000.

13.
Sea World and La Jolla

Sea World deserves a whole morning. Hit the gate before it opens and run, not walk, to the marvelous refrigerated indoor penguin exhibit so you can take the moving walkway through at least twice. After that, try the killer whale show. Then cover the other shows and exhibits as your fancy dictates. Feeding the marine animals tops our list of things to do now that I know not to dangle squid over the walrus! I dangled a squid so the walrus would open its mouth to improve the photograph; the walrus, having played, and won, this game before, squirted a mouthful of rotten-smelling saltwater. My wife tried hard not to laugh, at least for a moment.

In the afternoon, you might want to head up the coast toward La Jolla or cross the bridge to Coronado that appeared under the credits on the TV show *Simon & Simon*. We enjoy the rocky coast up toward La Jolla's posh shopping—bring big bucks!

The Cliff Walk around La Jolla Cove's a popular spot to watch the surfers. It was the setting for the finale of *It's a Mad, Mad, Mad, Mad World.* The Scripps Institute of Oceanography Aquarium offers a more intellectual approach to exhibits than Sea World does.

The sneaker trip for adventurous folks here is a two-person hang-glider soar off the bluffs. The timid or sensible can watch the gliders above Baker's Beach. Check restaurants as you walk through town and book a reservation so you can enjoy quality food in spots such as the Di Canti (Italian food).

The La Jolla Museum of Contemporary Art features Minimal, California, Pop, and other contemporary artists. Check on the La Jolla Chamber Music Society and Playhouse. Both offer quality works in lovely surroundings. The Playhouse was started by Cary Grant and often features famous movie stars.

Then, you might want to drive out past Ocean Beach to Sunset Cliffs and watch the sunset from the Cabrillo National Monument on Point Loma. This is a fine site from which to photograph San Diego or to watch for whales from December through February.

For more information:
Sea World, 619-226-3901.

14.

Southern California Classic Cars

Southern Californians live in cars—that's the result of massive freeways. They also die in them—75-mph bumper-to-bumper traffic yields some massive crashes. So your car of choice supposedly reflects your income, status, and sex appeal. Given this, it's not surprising that some of the best auto museums anywhere are in Southern California, where so many auto manufacturers test new design ideas on the street and by the beach.

There's a chance to drive your own, too. Several firms rent classic cars of seniors' salad days and spiffy vehicles that appear in movies or on TV.

Merle Norman Classic Beauty Collection: Cosmetics obviously pay off. If your tastes run to gleaming marble and gold leaf, you'll adore this wonderful, little-known museum. While only about thirty of the hundred and thirty classic and antique cars in this fabulous collection grace the lavishly decorated, marble-floored showroom at a time, a great many are "celebrity cars." Like movie stars?

Rudolph Valentino's 1923 Qvions Voisin and Fatty Arbuckle's scarlet 1923 McFarlan Knickerbocker Cabriolet are usually on display.

An outstanding collection of over eleven hundred hood ornaments lurks on the mezzanine, and your two-hour tour (offered twice daily) also includes a hubbub of often loud and definitely unique mechanical musical instruments. One of the staff calls this "Merle's No-Man Band." Write or call ahead: Merle Norman Classic Beauty Collection, 15180 Bledsoe Street, Sylmar, CA 91243, 818-367-2251.

Los Angeles County Museum of Natural History: The ground-floor car hall of the largest natural-history museum in the West offers a rotating exhibit of automobiles appropriate to "the city of wheels." There's lots of parking in Exposition Park, and the museum is open Tuesdays through Sundays, from 10:00 A.M. to 5:00 P.M.

Car clubs sometimes hold meetings here or in the parking lot of the San Diego Auto Museum at the Del in Coronado (see below) so check the schedules.

San Diego Auto Museum: In Balboa Park, the San Diego Automotive Museum is another delight for Ford fanciers. A $150,000 grant from local Ford dealers ensured that there would be flotillas of Fords on hand. This is the place for the research-minded, with the complete book and manual collection of the Horseless Carriage Foundation and much else on hand. Last visit, we watched a silver-haired car buff from Chicago just about break into tears when handed the complete repair manual for his antique Buick. Another visitor lusted after an old Indian motorcycle "just like I rode in 1934."

RV owners should check on the custom designs. RVs weren't, after all, invented after WWII. You could make a case that a Conestoga Wagon, the white-topped conveyance that pioneers drove westward, was the first RV. At $4 for a museum ticket, it's a good value for auto buffs. San Diego Automotive Museum, 2080 Pan American Plaza, San Diego, CA 92101, 619-231-AUTO.

Deer Park: This small collection hides down the road from San Diego Champagne Boulevard and from Lawrence Welk's Mobile Home Community. As the owners also run a winery and delicatessen, many visitors buy lunch makings and enjoy the grassy picnic area. It's about a forty-five-minute drive from San Diego on the usual "convertible" day. This puts one in the mood for the twenty-two 1950s convertibles in the collection of seventy-five nice, but hardly perfect, cars in two buildings decorated in the style of 1920s' garages.

The 1953 "Triple" Black Cadillac reflects the $150,000 investment for lots and lots and lots of finish coats. A baby-blue 1957 Chevrolet Bel Aire convertible, some early Corvettes, an Indy race car, and a batch of others offer the car buff a decent half-day outing that combines nicely with a visit to the San Diego Wild Animal Park, a nearby eighteen-hundred-acre game preserve. Deer Park: Vintage Cars & Wines, 29013 Champagne Boulevard, Escondido, CA 92026, 619-749-1666. Admission; $4. Hours: 10:00 A.M. to 4:00 P.M. daily.

Rental Classics: After whetting your automobile appetite on museums, you might want to try one. National Rental Car, at the Los Angeles Airport, offers rental classics such as Karen Carpenter's old Chrysler 300H, various 1957 Chevrolet Bel Aire convertibles, "porthole" Thunderbirds, and much more. Reservations are recommended. Prices run $50 a day and up, plus 10 cents a mile and up.

Want to rent Magnum's Ferrari? Budget Rentals in Marina Del Rey, while defining oxymoron, offers this as well as cars from *Riptide*, *Matt Houston*, *Hunter*, and, for *Dynasty* buffs, the Carringtons' Rolls-Royce. Rentals run "in the low hundreds per day," plus mileage.

If you really get hooked on classics, California Custom Coach of Pasadena makes replica 1935 Auburn Speedsters and sells a wildly varied assortment of classic, old, and just plain succulent cars such as wire-wheel MGs and the like. It's open from 9:00 A.M. to 6:00 P.M. weekdays, Saturdays from noon to 4:00 P.M. California Custom Coach, 1285 East Colorado Boulevard, Pasadena, 818-796-4395.

You might see a movie star kicking the tires at Rodeo Coach in Beverly Hills. The company customizes "cars for the stars." A lot load of Ferraris, Excaliburs, Stutzes, Clenets, and other exotic irons is available and at least some come from movie- and TV-star owners. If you have to ask the price, you probably can't afford one! Rodeo Coach, 9501 Wilshire Boulevard, Beverly Hills, 213-278-5000.

15.

Escondido and the Million-Dollar Bass

Drive forty-five minutes to an hour north of San Diego to enjoy the Wild Animal Park in Escondido and see animals from the San Diego Zoo roaming in natural surroundings. The hour-long monorail tour around the park's perimeter rests your feet. Binoculars are sometimes needed on this trip when animals sulk at the opposite end of huge enclosures.

We found the most unusual sights in the enormous bird cages that were filled with tropical growth and beautiful macaws and other birds that fly within touching distance. All small-animal exhibits cluster around Nairobi Village, and the waterfowl in the lagoon fit our needs. Elephant, bird, or domestic dog and cat shows each last about thirty minutes.

You can expect to spend most of a day at the Wild Animal Park. We try to schedule trips so we can get into Lake Hughes for a bit of bass fishing. It's considered likely that the next world-record largemouth bass will be taken in these waters sometime between December and April. So if you're a bass type, give it a try.

If you don't fish, you might spend the evening in Escondido where a massive new theater/cultural center offers a nice mix of musicals, musicians, and drama. Also there's Lawrence Welk's.

As elsewhere in California, the key to artful outings is as simple as getting off the freeway and checking out the back roads that wind among the avocado orchards. Then, of course, there's El Camino Real's Missions.

Staged out at a day's ride's distance, the missions on the "Royal Road" run all the way north to San Francisco Solano. If you're staying in San Diego, as most visitors do, don't miss San Diego de Alcada, the first California Mission, at the southern terminus of El Camino Real. A visit here goes nicely with a trip to the Old Town State Park.

From Escondido, take a short detour over on Highway 76 to San Luis Rey de Francia. It's just east of Oceanside and is perhaps the most graceful California Mission of all.

San Juan Capistrano, known for the cliff swallows that return from Argentina on March 19, offers a wonderful 1777 chapel. It's just off Calle de Borrachos, or "drunk street," in the town of the same name and not far off the main inland route to Los Angeles.

For more information:

San Diego de Alcada, 10818 San Diego Mission Road, San Diego, CA, 619-281-8449.

San Luis Rey de Francia, 4050 Mission Street, San Luis Rey, CA, 619-757-3651.

San Juan Capistrano, Ortega Highway at Camino Capistrano, San Juan Capistrano, CA, 714-248-2049.

The Southern Sierras

16.

Real Rides—Southern Sierra Stock Drives

Horseback rides run from urban parks to Sierra pack trips. You can take a day ride at the Bonanza Ranch near Lake Tahoe or you can ride in Golden Gate Park or near the ocean in L.A. Equestrian lessons, from three-eventing through dressage to polo, abound. However, working rides offer a different perspective.

I learned this years back when we moved horses and cattle from California's Central Valley up into the Sierra pastures and pack stations. You still can find authentic trips such as these if you search.

One of the best is the spring or fall stock drives to and from the Sierras out of Rock Creek pack station near Bishop. They're not quite weekends—you need to arrive Friday, and the drive ends Tuesday at a banquet. They're not for those who've never been on a horse before. But if you are a riding buff or have a teenage daughter or other horse addict in the family, you'll score massive points with one of these trips.

Rides move stock between the Owens Valley and High Sierra. You need not be expert, but must have had some time in the saddle. You start early in the morning after a huge camp breakfast and end the ride early in the afternoon when it's still cool. There's time to rubberneck, fish, or simply rest.

Taking a chuck-wagon break

Logistics are easy. You turn up with duffels and a sleeping bag with air mattress and bring alcohol if you need it. The packer, who supplies a check list of things to bring, supplies tents, copious chuck-wagon food, ice, and snacks. Packers wangle the stock, set up the tents, offer riding lessons as needed, and make the trip a pleasure.

You get a horse and saddle that fit your needs and ability level. You also get picked up at either Bishop or Mammoth Lakes airports or the

Greyhound Bus station if you opt not to drive.

There's no better way to get an idea of the old trail rides than with a horse and cattle drive like this. It's a wonderful immersion into cowboy lore. Of course, other trips out of Rock Creek offer fall color and access high-country lakes. Like other packers, Rock Creek offers guided and unguided visits into the back country that are a wonderful introduction to the High Sierra.

For more information:

Rock Creek Pack Station, Box 248, Bishop, CA 93515. Summer phone, June 15 to October 1, 619-935-4493, winter phone, 619-872-8331.

17.

Mammoth Skiing

Mammoth Mountain is mammoth! Over a hundred and fifty trails served by gondolas, chair lifts, and T-bars suit skiers of every ability. Add the longest season in the Sierra—skiing runs to Memorial Day for sure, with snow even as late as the Fourth of July and, in big snow years, you can come close to year-round action. So it's easy to see why this resort attracts most "serious" SoCal skiers. Plenty of lodgings and more restaurants than anyone could try in a week complete the package. If you like big, you'll love Mammoth, and there's no question but that it's the best place to ski in California south of Lake Tahoe.

June Mountain, now known as Mammoth/June Ski Resort, offers over three hundred and five runs served by a school of lifts and a tram. It's a personal favorite, with its main lodge at midmountain and varied exposures that mean quality snow even in spring. The Children's Ski Center starts kids correctly while parents ski on their own to strike a blow for parent lib. Nearby Nordic and snow-play packages complete the picture.

Tamarack Lodge Resort offers quality cross-country track around six lakes and complete packages that include lodgings. Cross-country, of course, is the low risk way to take a first ski trip. Then, if you like, you can opt for downhill or snowboarding. The last is very, very quickly learned by surfers and other suntanned L.A. types.

The drive's a reasonable evening's run from L.A. if you don't stop for dinner. We used to party until late and then drive until dawn to hit the slopes. Sleep in the car, have a buddy in the ticket office, and then even college kids can manage the prices. Otherwise, I'd consider a cost-cutting package that might include lodging, lift tickets, and, hopefully, condos where you can save massive amounts by preparing simple food. Tip: Bring a favorite stew from home.

You can't blame Mammoth for its lift-ticket prices, since about a third of this revenue goes to insurance. In the old days, skiers assumed the risk of slings and arrows. These days, sadly, such isn't the case. Fortunately, they offer all sorts of packages for kids skiing with adults, midweeks, and early and late skiing. These change from season to season, but early-season rates can save. I suggest you ski late in the year when the snow is good. We've skied as late as the April opener of trout action at Crowley. Skiing and trout fishing on the same day works for me. We've also done a bit of hang-gliding in the calm winds of early morning and scooted over to Mammoth early enough to ski until dark.

Do start with lessons and rentals. Then, if you find you enjoy snow action, you can buy gear at end-of-season sales. Late-season bargains are, after all, early season's "high tech."

For more information:
Mammoth Mountain Area, including Mammoth/June Ski Resort, Box 24, Mammoth Lakes, 93546, 619-934-2571.

18.

Lone Pine—Movies and Manzanar

I remember Lone Pine as the supply point for John Muir Trail backpacking, I was too young to remember Manzanar, but old enough to remember cowboy movies. So Lone Pine always looks familiar. It's still more than a stopover to Mammoth ski areas or Reno. It's a lovely spot to spend a weekend with road- and foot-access fishing, dandy birding, and a lot more. But for me, Lone Pine means movies and Manzanar.

Movies and the Alabama Hills: Long before movie budgets rivaled those of small nations, Hollywood folks would pack up and film the summer away in the Alabama Hills just out of Lone Pine. I asked John Wayne about this years back. He noted, "Well, son, it was cheap, but it was also a great place for us to fish on our time off." The Alabama Hills also deserve a look for their geology, as it's some of the Earth's oldest.

Now that "Film Classics" infest TV, even youngsters would appreciate seeing where the Lone Ranger got ambushed, where Roy Rogers found Trigger, or Tom Mix discovered Tony. Cowboy movies started here with Fatty Arbuckle's 1920 Western *The Roundup*. Big names strapped on guns here. Humphrey Bogart, Clint Eastwood, Gregory Peck, Jack Palance, Natalie Wood, Jack Lemmon, John Wayne . . . the list goes on. Recently, both Mel Gibson's *Maverick* and Alec Baldwin's *The Shadow* were filmed here.

Classics weren't limited to cowboys, either. *High Sierra*, *Charge of the Light Brigade*, and a batch of others were shot in and around the area that locals call "Movie Flats." You can even see shot markers to show where the cameras rolled.

Drivers can find the Movie Road that leads to all this north off the aptly named Picture Rocks Circle that runs on Whitney Portal Road before cutting south and circling back to its start. There are at least fifty natural rock sculptures along the road, too. Some are marked; others are not. Kids seem to adore imagining their own animals to see if they match up with mileage-marked rocks such as Batman, bullfrog, walrus, or hambone.

The Shame of Manzanar: You can make a decent case that the Civil Rights advances of the Supreme Court could have come out of Chief Justice Earl Warren's feelings about his actions as California attorney general and the actions of the federal government when thousands of Japanese Americans were relocated from Southern California to the internment camp at Manzanar. It's a place to visit if only to see the bare remains—two sentry posts, the auditorium, and the cemetery—and to understand why this should never happen again. There's more information in the Eastern California Museum in nearby Independence.

We visit here, leave flowers in the cemetery, and then move on to something cheery such as catching a fish.

19.

Chugging California's Highest High

Since so many Southern Californians roller-blade, bike, hike, or otherwise ensure hard bodies, I've added a test that's a step up from bikini boogie on the Venice boardwalk. I did this trip in a day in my salad years. Many do it in a weekend now. Many more turn good intentions into a quick retreat back down Mount Whitney. Ball's in your court. Hit it if you can.

The Mount Whitney Trail runs from Whitney Portal up to Mount Whitney. It tests frisky folks who don't mind climbing over six thousand feet in just ten and seven-tenths miles to the highest peak in what Alaskans call "the lower forty-eight." The view, given a clear day and recent rain, is absolutely wonderful. According to a less-than-fit friend, "It's almost worth the climb." So it ranks in the "fun once," "I've done that" list for most backpackers, iron pumpers, et al.

Getting there is easy. You head thirteen miles west of Lone Pine on Whitney Portal Road. Finding a campground can be challenging, as sites, except the group campground (800-283-CAMP), aren't reserved. So drive up and take your chances and remember to park in the overnight area.

Getting up the trail isn't that hard from July through October when the snow's gone. It's the walk back that kills your hamstrings. If you've backpacked, you'll find it a decent test of your flat-land fitness. Up and back in a day can be rather a haul, so do some easy hikes first to test your boots, feet, and fitness. Then do some hikes at altitude. If you expect to stay at the top of the peak, bring warm gear. It's cold at night!

Don't overlook the chance of storms, either. Bring rainwear. Also, as there's no water up the hill, bring some and filter or boil. You can't light campfires, so bring a stove if you plan to stay overnight. In the last case, you need a wilderness permit. If you hike it early, you even may need ice axes. By now, sensible folks will be considering a weekend in a Lone Pine motel, but those who like challenges will be checking gear. In either case, remember that you heard it here that it's over six thousand feet vertical.

For more information:

Mount Whitney District, Box 8, Lone Pine, CA 93545, 619-876-5542.

Maps: USGS 15-minute quads: Mount Whitney and Lone Pine (these look nice on the "I love me" wall to remind you not to do it again).

20.

Lake Isabella—Southern California's Tahoe

Since it's the largest freshwater lake in Southern California at 38,400 acres when full, it sometimes seems as popular as Tahoe. So you might try a spring or fall visit. The former finds green shores and a full lake and early-season anglers looking for bass. It's also a good time to try a whitewater raft trip on the lake's tributary, the Kern River. Spring also means exceptional wildflowers and decent birding that's best in wet years.

Fall visits find the lake down, the shore uncrowded and rather brown, but with a wonderful sense of quiet (except during deer season). We're particularly fond of mushroom picking—not for the less-than-expert—in mild years with wet falls and late freezes.

Summers run to water-skiers, high-speed bass and other boom boats. It's a good time to head to higher-elevation waters such as the June Lake Loop or Twin Lakes near Bridgeport.

Winter's abandoned save for die-hard anglers, but the twenty-five-hundred-foot elevation keeps snow away. If you take your RV, winter can be prime time, as it's rarely cold enough to freeze and you're totally isolated in the same campgrounds that are mobbed in the summer.

As the lake's a typical "two-story" impoundment with cold water deep, it gets heavily stocked with trout all year. This fattens up the black bass that, according to experts, eat about half of the stocked trout and grow to nearly twenty pounds. There's good crappie, bass, and bluegill fishing, too.

However, the lake offers far more than fishing. Water-skiing is popular all summer. There are dandy shoreline campgrounds and decent picnic areas for those who drive the forty-five miles up Highway 178 from Bakersfield. If you've been in Bakersfield, you know how hot it gets, and should have no trouble imagining the lake's popularity!

The Kern River's a wonderful spring-rafting venue if you go with pros and ignore Merle Haggard's "I'll Never Swim the Kern Again" song. The Kern River is also a dandy spot to fish and camp. There are a huge number of nearby streams to fish.

However, we see Isabella as a wonderful spring or fall destination and, in a mild winter, a nice spot where you can avoid the snow. It's also a decent stopover and easy drive from L.A. for those who might go onto the Giant Sequoias, Kings Canyon, or Yosemite. About the only drawback is the spring wind which can blow boaters off the lake and muddy up its water. So check the forecasts and realize wind is the reason why there's an eleven-foot minimum on boats on the lake.

For more information:

Sequoia National Forest, Isabella Lake, 619-379-5646.

North Fork Marina, 619-376-3241.

Coast Range and Island Attractions

21.

Odd in Ojai

I discovered the Ojai Foundation years ago when hired by a New York advertising agency to write an article about an African-American TV starlet joining an Indian tribe at a sweat-lodge ceremony. A few problems came up. The Indians showed up eight hours late; it rained; and the "authentic" sweat lodge turned out to be a PVC dome covered with plastic. (Note: I got the article anyway, but have buried most of its memories in the "never again" department.)

However, even after ten years I can forget neither the site of the Ojai Foundation at the top of its two ridges far above the Ojai Valley nor its people, who defined Zen calm when the PR types, agents, hairdressers, drivers, TV stars, makeup artists, cameramen, and everyone else around them lost their cool and roared back down the rutted dirt road to Hollywood and home.

I remember the quiet as I waited for my ride to return, watching red-tailed hawks soar along the ridges. If you didn't look to the west toward scenic Ojai, you had a sense of California as it was. You still can get this sense of timelessness, of the spirit world, and of self at the Ojai Foundations, retreats.

This isn't anything new. Setukim, the site of the foundation, started with a cluster of tents in 1927 as a unique educational center and nonsectarian, self-sustaining, and environmentally concerned community. This was far before these views became politically correct. Over the years, it's evolved into a teaching center where urban kids and their teachers can find peace and, in some cases, a sense of fulfillment. It's also a spot where you can regain a new sense of California as it was and yourself as you'd like to be.

Today, the road up the hill's a bit better and the yurts—classic domed wall tents of the Mongols—are available to individuals, couples, families, or groups, at $35 a night, for retreats. Just bring your own food, a cooler, and bedding.

You can join the staff at meditations or not. You can help in the garden, hike the trails, try the kiva or sweat lodge—they've a new, authentic model—or simply contemplate the hawks. It's a quiet place where you sometimes find leaders to take you to new places of the spirit and sometimes find that your own spirit, freed from urban and work pressures, soars with the hawks.

Just park your car for the weekend and leave the cellular phones at home.

For more information:

The Ojai Foundation, 9739 Highway 150, Ojai, CA 93023, 805-646-8343.

22.

Santa Ynez Valley—California As It Was

Ever since we got stuck on a muddy road high in the Santa Ynez Mountains and had to camp in a State Park restroom—it's more comfortable to set sleeping bags on the wooden slats in the shower than on the concrete—I've had a fondness for the Santa Ynez Valley. When seven of us chugged out off the mountains, a local rancher let us make calls, take showers, wash and dry clothing, finish the family stew, and track mud everywhere. It was, and is, that kind of hospitable place.

The valley reminds me of the long-gone days of the Napa Valley, when wineries were small, tasting informal, and trips without traffic. For, while the "discovery" of Santa Ynez as a wine-growing region dates to about 1969, it's clear that three Spanish missionaries, as is usually the case, knew in what conditions grapes would grow and exactly where this could be found. These days, you can tour twenty-eight wineries (see Solvang, Chapter 25) and enjoy a host of other activities.

I see this as a spring or fall vacation. In the spring, fields are green, wildflowers bright, and young foals tap along with their dams in the lush grass. Fishing's good in Lake Cachuma, and that's some of the best bass fishing in California, and there's superior picnicking around Santa Barbara's water hole.

Horses are a major interest in the valley of the Santa Ynez. Standard and even the odd miniature race along white wood rails, but it's thoroughbred race horses and Arabians that glue me to the binoculars. Kids will like the miniature-horse farm, Quicksilver. Ask about the carriage-driving contests and the Santa Barbara-area polo for the Rolls set.

Every now and then, you'll see oddments such as llamas—"llama mammas" in the spring. Add the "chi-ca-go" of the California quail and their alarm calls as red-tailed hawks circle high in the sky where, in my long-gone salad days, California condors sailed.

Cachuma Lake: Fishing and cruising Cachuma Lake offers its own pleasures. During winter, active trout-planting programs keep anglers happy and bald eagles fed. Eagles from the Northwest, which manage nicely on Alaskan salmon during the summer, follow sensible snow birds down to Cachuma. Eagle cruises aboard the *Osprey*, a forty-eight-foot tour boat, let you watch the eagles that use their "eagle eyes" to spot stupid "truck trout" near the surface, swoop down, and grab dinner. Bring a long (300-500mm) lens and fast film for eagle shots, as boats don't go so close that they frighten these wonderful birds.

You get much closer to mallards, herons, ospreys, and other birds as well as deer and the odd raccoon or coyote. You probably won't see mountain lions and bobcats, but they're there.

The fishing in Cachuma Lake, which borders Highway 154—a sensible, if slow, cutoff from Highway 101—divides by season. Winter's trout time; spring and fall offer bass, panfish, and some trout. Boat rentals improve catches in summer with its slower action. Do visit Nojoqui Falls, which flows most of the year; its green cliffs host all sorts of birds in the summer.

Fall finds ducks, rain that turns summer-browned hills green, and an almost total absence of visitors—except for Solvang's Danish Days in mid-September. Fall's a favorite time to relax, enjoy a bike ride or hike, take a boat ride on the lake, or tour vineyards during the harvest.

Valley Villages: Small towns such as Ballard, with its wonderful inn, restaurant, and private school, or Los Olivos, with its art galleries and wine shops, delight all year. So does Santa Ynez with its Old Town Museum and Carriage House. No matter the season, there's something going on in Solvang or in nearby Santa Barbara, but one weekend here is like one kiss that sends you back for more.

23.
Catalina Considered

Some experts believe that the last mammoths in North America lived here. So Catalina's history goes way, way back. Cabrillo got here first in 1542, and a couple of hundred years later, Yankee smugglers and Russians with their Aleut sea-otter hunters hid from Mexican customs here.

By 1880, the island of Catalina was the posh watering hole for Southern California society and after William Wrigley Jr. of chewing gum fame bought the whole place, Avalon became a fishing mecca. The famous Avalon Tuna Club set record standards for successors such as the International Game Fish Association, and an interesting mix of Hollywood stars and celebrities including Winston Churchill turned up. What one wag called the "Pasadena Posh People" put in a tricky little nine-hole golf course you can still play. Topography and lack of water prohibited a full course.

The famous Avalon Ballroom attracted big bands between the "war to end all wars" and the next one. These days, the island's changed less than most of the California Coast. It costs a mint to build, and the California Conservancy has owned eighty percent of the land since 1975. So visitors enjoy an island time machine that sits in what many feel is the best climate in America. No weather, just climate!

While you can do the over-and-back, Catalina cries out for a weekend or, better, extended midweek stay. On weekends, the Catalina Express has runs from Long Beach, Catalina Cruises promises the lowest fares, and both commuter plane and helicopters from Long Beach near the *Queen Mary* buzz back and forth. From 9:00 A.M. to sundown,

Avalon or, at the other end of the island, Two Harbors get lots of visitors who rush off in search of fun and sun.

Another set of aquatic folks crowds their sail and power craft into Avalon and Two Harbors in search of moorings that often fill early in Emerald Bay, Howland's Landing, and Fourth of July or Cherry Coves. Then they need to anchor out if, in fact, they remembered to bring three hundred feet of anchor rope. Boaters are ideally set up to enjoy the superior diving off the island. (Note: There are dozens of snorkel and dive shops, safaris, and outings offered on the reefs, rocks, and wrecks around the island.)

You also can rent inflatable, sit-on-top or advanced cruising kayaks, small sailboats, power boats for skiing and such, and various personal watercraft; you also can jet ski, parasail, or, for the less adventurous, take a ride on the new Starlight "semisubmersible," a glorified glass-bottom boat. We like the night cruise. Other cruises head out to watch flying fish, look for whales, or got to Seal Rocks; or aim for twilight dining at Two Harbors. We take it easy on the beach. There's lots to do and some extremely fit folks to watch as they play volleyball and such in—at least most of the time—amazingly skimpy bathing suits.

You can fish, too. Shore and pier fishing with light gear offer a mix of small fish. Charter boats that take you out into the kelp expand your piscatorial opportunities, and you can rent tackle. You can book the above near the dock where the tour boats unload.

On land, newcomers to the island should take a Catalina shuttle bus that runs between Avalon and Two Harbors, with stops at trails, camps, and other attractions, or consider the Skyline Drive tour along the islands' "dinosaurian" backbone. If the hills of Avalon make your dogs bark, save your feet with a rented gas-powered golf cart under the Holly Hill House or sit out the Avalon Scenic Tour.

Hikers find some of the best trails in California lead down to deserted coves and quiet rocky beaches. Just remember the trail back up is much, much steeper! In town, a special tour of the old casino and its well-known ballroom and theater and a trip to the museum deserve a couple of hours during the middle of the day when it's a bit hot to fry around the pool.

Of course, all visitors shop and eat. It's a Catalina rule that you've got to have something edible, and often melting, in one hand. Ice cream in waffle cones, cotton candy, corn dogs, snow cones, squid or clam chowder, hot dogs, and other plain-to-just-plain, no-apology-needed, junk food is everywhere. Stands, al fresco gardens, water-view streets, deck or patio dining let you complete your suntan . . . or burn. Did we mention the need for a brimmed hat, sunblock, and sunglasses, comfortable light clothing, and very, very comfortable walking shoes?

We stay in bed and breakfasts or hotels with continental and bigger breakfasts. We usually graze our way around town during the day as we time our peripatetic munchies with the "ins and outs" of shops that sell everything from the smallest swim suits this side of Rio to museum-quality scrimshaw carved on fossil walrus tusks. This means I spend a lot of time outside shops with two cones in hand.

Granted, a considerable number of shops specialize in T-shirts for those who need a reminder of where they've been. (Well, maybe not—if that were the case, the print would be upside down.) But there are enough shops with quality merchandise, such as Gulls and Buoys, our favorite clothing shop, to put heavy hurt on your plastic. Catalina Gold Company has, according to my wife, "wonderful jewelry," and the Perico Gallery runs to nice watercolors and drawings and the famous Catalina Bird Tile Collection. If you insist on T-shirts, try Catalina's by the Sea for shirts up to XXL and all sorts of affordable stuff.

Come evening, it's time to put on the glad rags and dine out. It's disgustingly romantic here, so you'll find hordes of newlyweds, or newly attracteds, wandering about. You can even, for $50, put your own names on a brick along a walk in town. (Given the California divorce rate, I'd ask about removal of same on need.) We like restaurants such as the Blue Parrot or Villa Portofino, but there's a wide choice—and fish deserve your full attention.

There's an even wider choice of lodgings that starts with campsite rentals, wall tents, and teepees and runs up through packages that might include your boat ride, transfers, lodgings, and champagne at a place like the Seaport Village Inn, where it could be $50 for two days/one night Sunday to Thursday, $69 for three days/two nights, or $89 for three-day/two-night weekends all the way to private rental villas with their own secluded pools for those who don't like tan lines.

Most lodgings offer transport for diving gear, shuttles, and much more. As a rule, prices rise as you near the water—if you've walked up four blocks to the top of the hill after a long swim, you find out why.

Given the bargains of midweek and off-season visits and the same-all-year weather, Catalina shines as an off-season getaway for singles, a great retreat for lovers, and a decent family destination for those with today's semiaquatic kids.

For more information:
Catalina Island Chamber of Commerce and Visitors Bureau, Box 217, Avalon, CA 90704 (on the Green Pleasure Pier), 310-510-1520.

24.

Santa Barbara: California's Riviera

Red-tile roofs arch over white walls and march up the hills behind Santa Barbara's pristine beaches. It's California's Riviera, a pristine place where old money gathers to spend its declining years amid an outstanding collection of small museums and wonderful restaurants. Mission Santa Barbara, the tenth mission in the chain that marches north to Sonoma, sets the theme for the town it overlooks. The original was destroyed by a 1925 earthquake, but the replacement entirely reflects the early pattern of the mission, an ancient Latin chapel in pre-Christian Rome. More than any other, the mission contains a vast collection of historical material. If you visit on Sunday, plan to attend services.

The Presidio of Santa Barbara, the last military outpost built by Spain in the New World, is now a state park and well worth a visit. Also check out the Historical Museum and Covarrubias Adobe. Add the Karpeles Manuscript Library and Museum with its manuscripts of famous authors and other historical figures, the Museum of Art, the Natural History Museum with its marine ecology demonstrations, and the Sea Center on the Pier, and you have a wonderful destination even for a rainy weekend.

The municipal architecture downtown, the wonderful shopping arcades, the "red-tile" tour of

Marker for the El Camino Real "King's Highway" in Santa Barbara

classic homes and buildings, world-class shops, good theater and all the amenities you would expect at the world's best destinations make Santa Barbara a wonderful place anytime except Easter when, like Balboa, it fills with vacationing college students. Christmas might seem like an odd time to visit a California coastal community, but the decorations, the lights, and the ambiance peak then. Shoppers' tip: Sales after Christmas offer massive savings.

If the weather's fair, consider a hike, a whale-watching cruise, or beach biking. You can roll along the harbor and around the Andree Clark Bird Refuge. The city sells a dandy bike map, *Pedal Around Town,* and rentals are available. There's a nice snack at the East Beach Grill to end your trip. Snacks seem the name of the game in Santa Barbara. There are so many interesting delis, cafes, shops, and food stands that we tend to graze around town, eating bigger meals at breakfast and lunch; then, if it's nice, we brown-bag dinner on the beach or pier.

Walk on out Stearns Wharf or through the botanical gardens to work off breakfast, snacks, lunch, tea, or dinner or do some windsurfing, surfing, or roller-blading—rentals and lessons available. Pickup volleyball at the beach, lazing by the Biltmore's pool, or simply sitting on the pier watching the sunset can fill your days, too.

Lodgings range from the usual chains to the classic tile-roofed Biltmore that's stood on the beach since 1927. You also can camp on the beach. Gaviota State Park, Refugio State Beach, El Capitan State Beach north of Santa Barbara, Carpinteria State Beach, Hobson County Park, Faria Country Park, and others offer a choice of spots. Getting camping reservations is the trick—you need to check through the state system for reservations two days to eight weeks ahead. You ask for reservations for a primary campground and two alternatives and take what you can get. Tip: Off-season or Sunday through Thursday visits improve your chances.

For more information:

Santa Barbara Conference and Visitors Bureau, 510 State Street, Suite A, Santa Barbara, CA 93101, 805-966-9222 or 800-342-5613.

25.

Solvang's Danish Delights

I've had a fond place in my heart for Danes ever since my first Victor Borge concert far too many years ago. Danes also gave us Hans Christian Andersen and the Tivoli, the first and I think still the best theme park. Then there's the open-faced sandwich and Danish pastry. However, it's useful to remember that Danes were tough enough to send their Jews to Sweden rather than turning them over to the Germans in WWII and were smart enough to move out of the Midwest winters to the beautiful Santa Ynez Valley in Southern California way back in 1911, long before the mass migrations after WWII.

Solvang's the happy result. Sure it's a tourist town, but long before Uncle Walt thought of Disneyland, folks here—and there's still sixty percent Danish heritage—meant it when they said, "Velkommen to Solvang." It's just a great place to spend a weekend. Why? Let us count the ways.

First, the architecture features the kind of timber-framed, cross-beam construction used on Danish farmhouses, and this is reflected in high points like the Tivoli Inn, various windmills, and some superior hotels and wonderful b and bs such as the Storybook Inn, which has a fireplace in every room and jacuzzis in a couple. Add rooftop storks and all sorts of other decorative oddments.

Second, the food can kill any diet. The many, many Danish bakeries and cafes begin the day with more kinds of bearclaws than Goldilocks found.

The Danes invented smorgasbords (my wife says this means "smeared with butter," and I know that's not true, even if it's accurate). Then there are the Danish dinners. "Diets" here mean having only one cooky. Caution: If you are dieting, don't visit from March 17 to 19 during "A Taste of Solvang," a weeklong festival with the World's Largest Danish and a Dessert Showcase to sample, provided you have already survived what they call the Walking Smorgasbord, where you buy a ticket and eat your way through town. I haven't been this full even on cruise ships!

Third, the shopping runs to lots of Dansk and our favorite Danish designs. Add Danish sweaters, a host of china, stainless, silver, and more right in town. Then compound things with the Victorian Shopping Village, Christmas Shop, factory outlets with "up to sixty percent off," and you'll have lots to tote home. Tip: Wait for the after-Christmas sales and never, never loan your spouse your plastic.

Fourth, the cleanliness makes everything special and says something about the way America's streets and sidewalks have slummed down in the last forty years.

Fifth, there's the Mission. Santa Ynez Mission is right off Copenhagen Drive and across the street from the Hans Christian Andersen Museum. Incidentally, the Evlerhoy Museum over on Attendag Road can show you more than anyone needs to know about Solvang's history.

Sixth, there's the wine. The Santa Ynez Valley was a prime wine-growing area back in Mission Days. There are at least twenty-eight wineries from Santa Maria down to Los Cruces. Most of these are on back roads and worth finding. Maps are available in town. It's Napa Valley without crowds.

Seventh, there are the toilets. While this is rather indelicate, as a travel and food writer I sometimes wonder where they hide the facilities—especially after wine tours where we use the designated-driver system on the Santa Ynez Valley Wine Trail.

Eighth, there's the entertainment. The Pacific Conservatory of Performing Arts (PCPA) offers wonderful performances in a Shakespearelike outdoor Festival Theatre. There is storytelling and all sorts of other activities.

Ninth, there's the golf and gambling. Superior courses such as La Purisima, rated #2 in California by *California Golf Magazine,* take advantage of the nifty weather. The River Course on the Santa Ynez River deserves a second day while the nongolfers shop. Gamblers can find the Santa Ynez Indian Casino on the Chumash Indian Reservation.

Tenth, and the most important reason, there are the people. Solvang's a friendly place; folks are glad to see you; prices seem fair, and you don't find that "come, spend, go" attitude too common in many tourist areas. It must be all that Danish pastry. How could anyone be mean after a daily Danish?

For more information:

Solvang Conference & Visitors Bureau, Box 70, Solvang, CA 93465, 800-468-6765.

PCPA, 800-549-PCPA.

La Purisima Golf Course, 805-735-8395.

Santa Ynez Valley Wine Trail, 800-824-8584.

Santa Ynez Indian Casino, 800-728-9997.

The Desert

26.

Lake Havasu

Lake Havasu offers wonderful fishing, nifty houseboats, quality camping, some of the best water-skiing in California and, during the summer, a world-class collection of hard-body water skiers in minimal attire. It's enough to make one invest in those expensive binoculars some insist they buy for birding. About the only drawback, aside from summer's heat, is getting there. It's grim across the desert even if you stay on the California side instead of heading for Parker in Arizona.

By the time the Colorado River gets down to Havasu, it's been through enough dams to filter out the silt and brown water that can be problems upstream. As a result, the water's clear blue, the fishing's good, and the late-fall-to-winter camping's better than that.

Lake Havasu City has the best amenities of the area, although some favor Parker City, and there are at least ten major marinas on both sides of the lake. When we visit during the cool of spring or fall, we hit the super to stock up for the boat-in campgrounds on the Arizona side of the lake that we favor. Otherwise, we stay at the Havasu Hot Springs Resort. If you don't own a boat, this is an excellent spot to rent one. Houseboats, fishing skiffs, ski boats, and even canoes at the upstream "riverlike" section of the lake offer a host of choices.

Fishing's scattered for much of the warmer part of the year, but stripers head up toward the river in spring and drop back down to Parker Dam in the fall. So even if you have a boat, the best bet is to hire a local guide to help locate the fish. However, if you simply want to catch catfish, black bass, or stray stripers with bait off the bank, you can set up just about anywhere. Add a cooler, an umbrella, and that pair of binoculars for watching birds of all types, and it's easy to laze away the day.

At night, it's just a short trip to Nevada—we hit Vegas for the shows—or the country-and-western nightlife in Parker or Lake Havasu City. If you visit in the late fall and camp away from the resorts, you'll find the black, star-studded sky entertaining. These days, with so much space junk up there, you can usually see a satellite or two every hour. Add the quiet of the lake, coyote and bird noises, and you know you're not in L.A.!

For more information:
Lake Havasu Chamber of Commerce, 602-855-4115.

27.

California's Lowest Low—Death Valley

Death Valley's Furnace Creek Hotel has to be the lowest, as well as one of the nicest, hotels this side of Israel. If deserts are your thing, Death Valley's the spot. Badwater's the lowest point in the Western Hemisphere at two hundred and eighty-two feet. The Borax Museum will show you more than anyone needs to know about Borax, "48 mule team," and otherwise. The Indian baskets and mining displays deserve a look. Add Scotty's Castle (an elaborate stone dwelling that was the result of an elaborate joke), the Amargoda Opera House (suppose you opened an opera house in the boondocks), and the mineral hot baths in Tecopa, and you've got a very weird winter weekend.

Petroglyphs

Summer? Don't even consider it. Temperatures top 125 degrees. In the old days, you could survive if you got stranded by drinking radiator water. Antifreeze won't make it. Late fall, winter if it's not raining, and early spring are the times to go—if it's not raining. Given this, you'll survive, even enjoy the trip.

Spring works. For example, in the last wet year, 1995, the lavender, purple, and pink wild flowers covered the hills from Lone Pine in the Owens Valley over the Panamint Range through Panamint

Springs (camping and a trailer park) in the Panamint Valley and down into Stovepipe and the aptly named Death Valley.

What makes this so spectacular, aside from the arid desert joys, is the short distance between America's highest and lowest points. Schedule your trip for a dusk view of Mount Whitney and the fourteen peaks around it that top 14,000 feet up from the valley that's below sea level, and you get an idea why the Sierras deserve John Muir's *Range of Light*. It's also a place to see if only as testimony to California's diversity.

For more information:
Death Valley Chamber of Commerce, 619-852-4524.

28.

Better in Barstow

Barstow sits on the banks of the Mohave River where, at least some of the time, there's a little water. The area's always been a crossroads since prehistoric man ambushed animals here starting at least fifty thousand years ago and extending up to drying of the massive lakes in the area's pluvial period. But Barstow got started with the railroad in 1853—it even took the middle name of William Barstow Strong, the tenth president of Santa Fe Railroad. The town now supports both the Union Pacific Railroad and the A, T & S F Railroad.

That seems appropriate, since one of the main attractions is the historic station and associated Harvey House that contain a bus terminal, shops, and, appropriately enough, a restaurant where "Harvey Girls" serve train passengers during short meal stops.

Highway buffs can enjoy old U.S. Route 66 that runs right down main street just a bit from the railroad. This historic route, the first decent all-year road across the U.S., is still popular with fans of the TV show of the same name and old-car buffs that race through once a year.

There's a major off-road vehicle area over in nearby Stoddard Valley and, for those of more sedentary tastes, factory-outlet stores and downtown shopping. Kids can enjoy the largest indoor swimming pool in Southern California at the Virgil Swim Center. As with the rock-hounding and golf, the pool's a solid treat during the winter.

However, we find Calico Ghost Town to be the area's main attraction—except, of course, if you're a marine stationed at the Logistics Base where all sorts of military hardware sit out in the dry heat. You get there—how else?—by driving north on Ghost Town Road.

Calico offers a sense of the old gold- and silver-mining days without the facade of tourist attractions. Part of its appeal is the battered old false-front buildings leaning together as if for protection against the wide open spaces around Calico Dry Lake. The sage, open flats, and colorful, if desolate looking, mountains seem a fit frame for a town with more than its fair share of ghosts.

If you visit during the cooler months—a local claims that's November through February most years—you might like to camp. There's a dandy campground in Owl Canyon north of town via Irwin and Fossil Bed Roads near the excellent Rainbow Basin National Natural Landmark. The layer cake of colorful strata reaches its artistic peak just after a rain. You'll find other camps near Calico Ghost Town, and a major campground along Highway 59.

If you want to kick around in the desert, four-wheel-drive vehicles help, but remember to tote water. There are all sorts of old mines to explore and places to get stuck and enjoy the other dubious joys of those who favor the roadless lifestyle.

Local food runs to the quick and casual, but prices are reasonable, and the folks we met demonstrated the town's claim as the Home of the California Smile. It's a nice stop on a leisurely trip between L.A. and Las Vegas and a worthwhile weekend destination during cooler months.

29.

California's Salton Sea

The Salton Sea could be called California's "Accidental Ocean" as it, to the distress of the Los Angeles Water District, resulted from a one-time diversion of the Colorado River. Today, it slowly shrinks in low-rainfall years and its salinity increases—it's between twenty-five and thirty percent saltier than the Pacific Ocean now. In years such as the winter of 1994-1995, it's up and out of its 380-square-mile normal surface area. But in any year, it's a fabulous place to watch birds in the winter when the temperature's mild and there's fishing for talapia and covia, both introduced from saltwater.

While the fishing isn't as good as in years past because of a massive talapia die-off and problems with salinity, it improved with the exceptional run-off of 1995. Talapia, a popular aquaculture fish, offer prime fishing for those who use the special baits required by the species' vegetarian habits. Covia bring big-fish ocean action and will hit both cast and trolled lures and baits.

Even in its normal saline condition, the Salton Sea is worth a visit if only to view its millions of shore, water, and marsh birds. At least fifteen species of ducks, shore birds such as pipits and snipe, raptors, and a host of other species make it possible for you to see a million birds flying up from the Salton Sea's shore, strand, and marshes.

You can either stay in posh Palm Springs digs an hour away and drive over to the sea or consider camping. The Salton Sea State Recreational Area on the north shore has several hundred campgrounds. Some, like Headquarters Campground that requires reservations, run to ramadas for welcome shade and paved parking. Other campgrounds run to more primitive sites. Our favorites are the less-crowded Salt Creek or Bombay Beach campgrounds. Boaters prefer these because they can launch right from camp, and it's first come, first served.

However, very few spots are so weather-sensitive. If it's cold and windy or hot and windy, you might head over to Palm Springs, or you might go to the General Museum with its remnants of the days when Patton readied his troops for North Africa. When the winds howl, it can take the paint off the side of a car; and when it's hot here at over two hundred feet below sea level, the Palm Springs air-conditioned malls look very, very attractive.

In decent weather, a side trip to the date country of the Coachella Valley, a trip north into the Joshua Tree National Monument, west into the Anza Borrego State Park, the Living Desert Reserve, or the many attractions of Painted Canyon look best. So pay close attention to the weather, as eating dinner in a sandstorm isn't much fun.

For more information:
Salton Sea Recreation Area, 800-444-7275.

30.

Palm Springs—Hollywood's Backyard

Even though the first hotel in Palm Springs opened in 1889, it took several decades for the movie industry to mature and discover what one wag called "Hollywood's backyard." Swimming pools and then air conditioning let romance replace sweating out the day under a big fan. Today, a host of stars, former and current, own homes here. More visit. It's a great place for people-watchers.

Things really started to cook—an appropriate term if you've ever been in Palm Springs during the summer—when Charlie Farrel, an actor of dubious skills probably best known as the father on "My Little Margie," and Ralph Bellamy got kicked off the tennis courts at the El Mirador Hotel when Marlene Dietrich wanted to bat balls. In response, they started the Racket Club in 1932, and U2's Crosby used to pretend to be a bartender. Farrel had a fair tennis game, but better players such as Charlie Chaplin used to play here all winter.

Today, the Racket Club is mired in what can only be called a tacky neighborhood, but there are still tattered white stucco cottages named for Spencer Tracy, Joan Crawford, and Lucille Ball. Even better, you can laze by the pool where Marilyn Monroe was discovered back in 1948. All this comes at about $90 a night. (619-320-9346.)

The Estrella Inn's another spot where celebrities spawned. It's claimed that Franklin D. Roosevelt slept here, but, as rumor has it, apparently not with Eleanor. Clark Gable and Carole Lombard stayed here (they were married). So did a host of other stars.

However, the Ingleside, our favorite spot, didn't usually allow stars. Well, Howard Hughes did register here as Earl Martyn (the "y" seems a neat touch) while chasing and reportedly catching Ava Gardner. And Greta Garbo hid here after the premier of *Camille*. These days, stars shoal up here as well as at its lovely restaurant, Melvyn's Rooms, with Oriental rugs and such, and dinners are priced at about $75, including limo pickups for shoppers. (800-772-6655.)

There are a batch of other older, and now carefully reconditioned hotels where stars stayed, sometimes even with their spouses. So you might explore the side streets or ask about the "old days" as you wander Palm Springs. It's a break from the wonderful shopping and a chance to work off the calories. Do, if you shop, consider a late-spring visit: Prices are low during the start of the "off" season, and shops have, according to my wife who always flies with extra luggage, "wonderful sales of summer clothing."

In your spare time, you can consider the couple of dozen golf courses and hundreds of tennis courts or take a trip out into the desert. You can get high with the Palm Springs Aerial Tramway or balloon rides. Explore with horseback rides up Palm Springs Indian and other canyons or rent a Harley hog for that James Dean (the actor not the sausage fellow) look. And, there's much, much more.

For night life, check out the seasoned performers such as Kay Starr in the Fabulous Palm Springs Follies or look for stars hiding in dark glasses and slouch hats. You never know—I ran into Bob Hope in the restroom one trip. He looked great!

For more information:
Palm Springs Visitor Information Center, 800-347-7746.

CENTRAL CALIFORNIA

The Central Coast

31.

San Luis Obispo—A City for All Seasons

When Father Junipero Serra founded Mission San Luis Obispo de Tolosa in 1772, he demonstrated the exceptional care with which Spanish missionaries sited their string of missions that grew into the largest cities on the California coast. But even for the missionaries, San Luis (never San Louie!) Obispo offered a remarkable mix of weather, beach, and ocean. It's now a splendid vacation site midway between Los Angeles and San Francisco, an hour and a half from Monterey.

No mission town ever loses sight of its Spanish heritage, but San Luis preserves its past better than most. After all, the mission, where the red-tile roofs now so common in Southern California were developed, is a gem, looking better today than it did even twenty years ago. The combination of a concerned citizenry and good sense turned the downtown shopping area into a gem unmatched where suburban malls are the rule.

Mission Plaza Path, a meandering walk beside San Luis Creek, sprouts decks and restaurants along its course. Do stop at the Chamber of Commerce on the corner of Chorro and Hiquera for information on a selection of history walks and other activities and a fine map of the area. Across the square, the red brick County Museum, once a library, offers additional insights into the history of the town.

After the mission period, San Luis slumbered in the sun under its chain of peaks while providing foodstuffs for the forty-niners. With most of the lands suitable for grazing, it's long been a cattle-raising area and, as a result, the land kept its flavor better than the rest of the Coast.

During this period, trains loaded up for the long climb over the pass to Paso Robles on the main coastal route between San Francisco and Los Angeles, now followed by Highway 101.

While the railroad was being built, San Luis had the second largest Chinatown in California. Today, the Ah Louis Store, established over a hundred years ago, and Chinese restaurants just down the street are all that remain—Bing's is a local favorite.

With the shift to diesel locomotives after WWII, San Luis Obispo settled into a pace slower than the rest of the Coast. Most visitors used the city as a layover on trips between San Francisco and Los Angeles. Motels started here.

During this period, the pervasive influence of California Polytechnic Institute began to be felt. Once a men's college specializing in agricultural and hands-on engineering, the destiny of the school is linked with that of the town. Today, after a growth period starting in 1963, Cal Poly is the major employer in the area, and town-and-gown conflicts are not the problem you find in many cities. For example, the president of the student body is a member of the Chamber of Commerce, and Poly engineers built or designed much of the town as part of their training.

Poly Royal, the former annual get-together for Poly students that featured both the most sophisticated musical and cultural attractions and the bucolic pleasure of agricultural days, helped join normally disparate groups, but it's now been killed by the actions of those who confused fun with license. So today, it's the mutual consent of Poly faculty and students that's kept San Luis's traditional red-tile and white-wall look even in the newer areas.

Once you cover downtown with a special look at the Network and Creamery where historical buildings are successfully recycled into pleasant shopping centers, you might like to take a drive to Poly and enjoy a tour of the campus. My uncle, Harold Davidson, founded Poly Royal and headed the music department at Cal Poly for many years. He was one of only two living Americans to have a building, today's music building, named after him at a California State University. After you tour Poly, it's time to think about food and lodging.

While the Madonna Inn isn't to everyone's taste, it's not to be missed. If you like baroque, you'll love the theme rooms—caves, grottoes, and what some call Victorian-Brothel decor and the entirely outrageous dining and gift-shop areas. It's just a short drive south of town on Highway 101.

On your travels near San Luis, you'll doubtless notice many new vineyards. The missionaries made their own wine here, but it's taken many years, and an astronomical rise in land prices in the Napa and Sonoma Valley areas, to bring the industry back to its roots. Today, at wine shops in town or toward Arroyo Grande or Paso Robles, you can enjoy a fine selection and, in many cases, buy quality wines at reasonable prices from small outlets without enough volume to export.

After a day's traveling, clamming, golfing, tennis—there are many fine courts all over town and at the college—or just lazing in the sun, enjoy some of the ongoing activities here. Each Thursday night, the San Luis Obispo County Band performs in Mission Plaza, and on Sunday evenings, you can enjoy the International Folk Dance Club and, if you like, learn to folk dance.

Clearly, no matter what time of year you visit this "city for all seasons," you can expect the timeless joys of sand and surf that bring the regulars back to San Luis, a town that's kept in close touch with its past without giving up on its future.

For more information:
San Luis Obispo County Visitors & Conference Bureau, 800-634-1414.

32.

Life is a Beach—Avilla, Pismo, Port San Luis, and Morro Bay

Not far south of San Luis Obispo off Highway 101, you come to the Avila and Port San Luis turnoff. Avila, a tiny but typically California beach town, offers excellent summer swimming and the usual cotton-candy delights of summer. Fishing is good from the piers, and excellent access to offshore albacore and salmon can be had out of Port San Luis at the north end of the bay during the season. Try to schedule trips during reasonably flat days. If you're not "aquatic," you might check out the Avila Valley Barn's "u-pick" with free hay rides through the orchards. Sandwiches aren't bad there, either.

As you approach Avila, you pass Sycamore Mineral Springs, the upscale replacement for the old, battered spa I remember from the 1950s. It's worth a stop if only to tour the grounds, and its food emporium, the Gardens of Avila Restaurant, offers an eclectic menu. The fine golf course along the creek belongs to the San Luis Bay Inn, an exceptional hotel on the bluff over the bay. It combines with Morro Bay's course for a golfer's weekend. The inn's restaurant was good last visit.

Less-expensive lodgings are also available in downtown Avila—if Avila can be said to have a downtown! Most are a bit old and remind me of the beach movies and beach towns of the 1950s, but most are well maintained and still comfortable. There's a pier here and another over at Port San Luis. Mild surf makes this a good spot for beginners to learn to surf or boogie board.

To the south, in Pismo Beach, the clams that made the beach famous seem in short supply. Experts used to stick their forks into the sand from four inches to a foot deep as they kept an eye out for large waves that wash the unwary off their feet. Then they'd measure clams to see if they were legal. These days, the sea otters and, one suspects, overharvesting have thinned the clam population and closed some sections.

The beach is, however, quite safe, wonderfully wide for walks, and, on a sunny summer day, a nice place to fish or dig clams in a bathing suit and tennis shoes. Winter requires waders.

The dunes behind Pismo deserve special mention for the "vroom, vroom" set with beach buggies, sand rails and other arcane off-road two-, three- or four-wheel machines. This popular area gets lots of traffic from the power types, and the dunes here offer some spectacular ups and downs—also sideways and end-over-end if you're not skilled. Check on rentals and lessons.

If it's lunch or dinner time, try F. McLintocks Mercantile for salsa or BBQ. Their dinner house is top-rated! If it's morning, follow the locals to Old West Cinnamon Rolls, in business for twenty-nine years and in Pismo since 1981. There's a nice farmer's market Thursday and Friday afternoons. If you visit on the weekend, try nearby Arroyo Grande's market on Saturday around noon.

A flock of good bike and sports-car roads run back toward San Luis Obispo. These vary with pavement, so check at any of the San Luis Obispo bike shops for information on smooth rides. Rental bikes are available in Pismo or in San Luis. From Pismo Beach, you can travel south to the Lopez Lake turnoff and cut back to San Luis Obispo on a classic sports-car two-lane road past the airport. Lopez Lake offers winter bass fishing and seasonal campsites and boat rentals.

Combine a visit here with one to San Luis Obispo or a run up to San Simeon, and you've a solid weekend or three- or four-day destination.

For more information:
Morro Bay Chamber of Commerce, 800-231-0592.
San Luis Obispo County Visitors & Conference Bureau, 800-634-1414.
Hearst San Simeon Historical Monument, 800-446-PARK for reservations.
Pismo Beach Chamber of Commerce, 805-773-4382.

33.

Morro Bay

If you head west from San Luis down the line of volcanic plugs that terminates at Morro Bay, you find RV hookups and tent sites between the bay and the excellent public golf course. At least it's excellent if you can keep your ball on the fairways; hook and you may end up three fairways down the hill! There's wonderful produce at San Bernardo Farms and on Thursday and Friday afternoon, there are farmer's markets. If you bike, the sprawl of back roads toward Los Osos, a popular local retirement community, and up Highway 1 offer special delights.

The area takes its name from Morro Rock which protects the harbor and offers quality surfing at its north side when the surf's right. It's one of a series of attractive volcanic plugs left over from past eruptions.

If the surf's not too high, you can find Pismo clams here, too. There's perch fishing, a nice bird sanctuary, and decent motels and restaurants in this working commercial fishing port. Reliable weather and a chance to walk along the bay make this spot special.

We used to camp here often in the fall, winter, or spring. My brother and I would fish off the rocks. Mom would putter in camp or check out the small shops in town. Dad would either go offshore to fish or curse his way around a golf course. A good time!

Today, Morro Bay's grown, but hardly as much as most California beach towns. As it's almost exactly midway between San Francisco and Los Angeles, it's an excellent escape from either city. And, like San Luis Obispo, it's a convenient stopover on the scenic route of Highway 1 or El Camino Real, the faster but still better than Interstate 5 road that once followed the missions all the way to Sonoma.

For more information:

Pismo Beach Chamber of Commerce, 805-773-4382.

San Luis Bay Inn, at Avila Beach, 800-592-5982.

34.

Classic Cambria

Cambria retains the flavor of an old-time beach. Consider it Carmel before the tourists arrived or Mendocino in the 1960s. Cambria's such an inviting seaside community that you hesitate to spotlight it. Still, it's so special that it can't be overlooked, and it's exactly two hundred and thirty miles from either L.A. or San Francisco. As a weekend destination, it meshes nicely with San Simeon, just up the coast, or with Morro Bay and San Luis Obispo, just south.

However, it seems a shame not to come in, check in, and kick back to enjoy the calm, the history, and the scenery. Cambria's worked as a supply center for logging, whaling, and mining, and today has both dairy farming and ranching as well as a growing number of wineries and orchards. It's small enough to allow you to see the town in a half day, but large and sophisticated enough to have shops that offer more than T-shirts and towels.

If you enjoy history, check out the Santa Rosa Chapel, built around 1860, where they still hold candlelight weddings. You can admire the Shaw House from the Santa Rosa Chapel. Downtown offers a decent mix of shops and restaurants that serve everything from simple food to California haute cuisine. There's a small theater, vintage movie house, and a saloon to handle night life. Tip: The local seafood and lamb are outstanding, and the small wineries in the area deserve a visit. In fall, a fruit trail offers its pick-your-own delights.

Unlike most beach towns, Cambria has a nice background of shore sand, grassy transition, and pine-studded mountains without condos and confusion. You can check out the deer, turkeys, and other critters from vantage points near inns in the woods or on short walks. Ask the locals. You're in friendly country here, but paths and paved roads and quotas haven't clogged access. Shamel Park has picnicking and shore access.

More than anything else, Cambria's a beach town. Admittedly, Moonstone Beach runs to its namesake rocks, but the combination of rocky headlands and crashing surf reminds me of Point Lobos without the check-in station. Offshore, you'll see all sorts of seals and sea lions swimming with gray whales in season. Closer to the shore, in the kelp that offers excellent fishing for those who launch out of Leffingwell Landing, you'll spy furry sea otters cracking shellfish with rocks or snoozing with a kelp "belt" holding them in place.

Getting there's easy. The town's just far enough off Highway 1 to avoid traffic. Staying there's inexpensive with an assortment of inns, oceanfront motels, and nearby camping.

For more information:

Cambria Chamber of Commerce, 767 Main Street, Cambria, CA 93428, 805-927-3624.

35.

Legal Highs—A Sky-Diving Weekend

Sky diving isn't nearly as dangerous as, say, the L.A. Freeway on the night before a holiday. If it were that dangerous, none of the sky-diving businesses would last more than a few days. Businesses must be insured, and insurance underwriters aren't charitable.

Most of all, sky diving is freedom. It's incredibly thrilling at first, then awe and anticipation change to sheer delight as you discover its weightless delights. Some are satisfied with a single solo static line or tandem jump. Others move to the freedom of free-fall. Some specialize in target diving, where you try to land in a specific spot.

As a weekend for a thrill seeker, sky diving's tough to beat. Blue Sky Adventures, out of Paso Robles and conveniently midway between Los Angeles and San Francisco, runs one of the best programs in the state in an area where the winds are usually low and the surroundings pleasant. You're a half hour from San Luis Obispo, San Simeon or the beaches. Owner Dave Hughes was the British skydiving champion in 1986. He takes a relaxed British attitude and an efficient approach that stresses safety, such as automatic activation devices (AAD) on free-fall rigs, special chutes, and intensive training. You've got three choices.

The tandem program locks you into a rig with an instructor who handles details such as the plane exit and landing. You enjoy, at least after the first rush, nearly a minute of free fall. Then the chute opens four thousand feet above the ground to reduce what a buddy in the service calls "the pucker factor." Landings are super soft under the extra-large ram-air chute. Best of all, you can learn what you need to know about jumping in about thirty minutes. Tandem jumps suit those who have little time, have physical problems, or who are a bit timid.

Static-line jumps are the "Stand in the door, hook up, green light and go" approach used by the military, automatically opening your chute as you exit the plane at thirty-five hundred feet. A static line—hence the name—opens your chute, and you steer yourself into the landing area with radio instructions from your instructor. The jump offers about five to six minutes' air time. Since you're basically dumped out of the plane like cargo, you can learn basic air and landing skills in four or five hours. This is the usual first jump for beginners.

Accelerated free-fall is a safe and effective method to get you into free-fall fast and a major short cut to sky diving. In five to six hours, you learn individually or in a small group, so you don't forget basics like body position before your chute opens and you pull the rip cord. Also, when you pile out of the plane, two instructors dive with you. They help with your body position, correct any spins, and offer reassuring grins as needed. Then you pull the rip cord—the AAD device with the instructors there as backup—and, with radio help, glide your chute down from about forty-five hundred feet. A few of these, and you're ready to go on your own.

All three of these approaches come with video and still photos so you can replay the thrills and chills later. What a killer birthday or anniversary present, even for those who find it a one-time-only thrill. It's a trip!

For more information:

Blue Sky Adventures, 805-239-3483. (Note: ask about group rates.)

36.

San Simeon—Excess Celebrated

When George Hearst walked to California in 1850 it's certain that he never expected his son William to turn a losing newspaper, the *San Francisco Examiner*, into an international publishing empire. William Randolph, not to mention his granddaughter, Patricia Hearst, of Liberation Army fame, ran to excess of one kind or another. Depending on whose biography you believe, he rather fancied Hollywood stars, especially Marian Davies, and he certainly believed in a several-of-everything approach to collecting art and architecture.

Hearst Castle, a complex with a 165-room Mediterranean Revival manor and, for spill-over guests, three massive cottages, does represent the best work of California's first major woman architect, Julia Morgan, back in the 1920s. It also demonstrates that with enough money anything is possible—even carting chunks of major European antiquities up onto a peak overlooking the ocean.

There's a unique mix here. You find catsup and paper napkins on huge, historic old monastery tables, and a phone booth near some of the finest paintings and tapestries in the world. Hearst savaged whole rooms to find parts for his Pacific-view palace. In fact, he never got everything in the place—the estate still owns massive amounts of artwork that's stored. When William Randolph died in 1951 at age 88, the estate went to California. Today, it's one of the most popular attractions in the state even though it's a bit awkward to reach.

There are just too many options. You can bus down and back, try Amtrak into San Luis Obispo, or drive up or down Highway 1 to San Simeon and its turnoff. If you drive down, plan time at Big Sur and Point Lobos. One thing is certain: You need to reserve tickets far ahead for the general downstairs tour and, most especially, for the special extended tours upstairs.

Given enough time, my own travel choice would be Amtrak from the Bay Area, an overnight in San Luis Obispo, and a shuttle bus to and from the Castle.

Whatever you like in the line of art, architecture, or horticulture, you'll find it at San Simeon. The

Swimming pool

exterior pool's particularly nice, and the stonework and sculpture around the pool deserve closer attention than most pay to the details. A bit of research—try a book on Julia Morgan—and some preparation on the Castle will let you look at the estate's one hundred and twenty-three acres with knowledgeable eyes.

Don't miss this one. It's worth a three-day weekend, despite the trip and the confusion of group tours. Morning tours in the summer, when the fog's in and the mountain peak sticks up through the mists, give a sense of Italy and a feeling of what it must have been like when you could keep what you earned and excess was expected from the rich. Winter visits, particularly after storms clear the air, offer incredible vistas.

For more information:
Hearst San Simeon Historical Monument, 800-446-PARK for reservations.

37.

Big Sur

Big Sur really starts a bit south of Point Lobos and, like Highway 1, runs along the ocean-washed west shore of the Santa Lucia Mountains down toward San Luis Obispo. Even if you come from Southern California, you may find the best way to see Big Sur is the hour drive south from Monterey—the three winding hours north from San Luis Obispo, past San Simeon, have only the inside lane to recommend them. Bikers note: It's a long way to the surf, so watch the shoulders on this narrow, two-lane trip.

My Big Sur goes back to the 1950s when we filmed John Steinbeck's short story "Flight" here. A bit later, we monitored what was then the last remaining group of sea otters—now you can see otters in the Monterey Harbor. In the forty years since, this area's changed less than perhaps any other on the California coast. Part of this is due to its natural isolation; part relates to the influence of Los Padres National Forest, various state parks, and the Ventana Wilderness.

Big Sur, with its photogenic restaurants, wonderful redwoods, and lovely namesake river, is normally the choice for lunch. If you're old enough to remember bell bottoms, you may remember *The Sandpiper,* a not-too-bad movie filmed in Big Sur with Elizabeth Taylor and Richard Burton. The hour drive from Monterey takes a complete morning if you stop, and you should, at Point Lobos. Do reserve ahead lunch or lodgings.

Andrew Molera State Park is only a bit over twenty years old and the once overgrazed meadows along the lower Big Sur River now sport a wonderful collection of California poppies and other flowers that peak in the spring. The river's particularly nice to wade in and watch as it hosts a huge number of resident and, in fall and spring, migrating birds. Best of all, it's a walk-in park with a mile hike to two and a half miles of quiet beach. Ask about the old buildings of the Molera Rancheria.

Pfeiffer Beach, the most scenic part of Big Sur, runs to massive cliffs, sea stacks (nature's offshore rock castles), and huge dunes. The road in through the cypress is particularly scenic and the beach is often deserted and always attractive. There are a couple of hundred campsites open all year—reservations a must during summer.

However, the most unique attraction of the area is doubtless the Ventana Wilderness. Nearly one hundred thousand acres of rugged trees, rolling grasslands, and serious, if low altitude, "ups and downs" demonstrate that California's coastal ranges, such as the Santa Lucias, offer their own rewards. You need permits from the district ranger and a considered choice of season. "After fall rains, but before summer fire closures" was one expert's advice. We're particularly fond of Ventana when the Sierras are snowed in but, due to the coastal fogs that limit the range of redwoods, it's a temperate

Point Lobos State Reserve

Skip it on big holiday weekends unless you arrive very, very early or you want to try some diving in Whaler's Cove. Permits are required, and access is limited to this most accessible California headlands. Even the forest fire that stripped a lot of vegetation in the middle 1980s helped the vistas, not that they needed much help. This is the kind of place that Kodak should support, as it's overrun with photographers anxious to duplicate the works of Brett Weston or Ansel Adams, who often photographed here. Note: Photographers and hikers must stay on the roped trails so they don't trample the plants.

If you can, park and walk. The park's only got five hundred and forty-four land acres, plus the seven hundred and fifty submerged acres added in 1960 when Point Lobos became the first underwater park in the U.S. So it doesn't take much to see everything and, on your own feet, you have the time to savor the sights without RVs stacking up behind you.

Even better, bring foul-weather gear and hope for rain. Point Lobos peaks when storms lash the shore, winds whip the cypress trees, and the tourists stay in Monterey. So winter visits are highly recommended; spring's the next best season; fall, particularly after the last rains, is okay and summer's a "skip it." Sad, but that's the price of Monterey Peninsula popularity.

place to backpack even in the middle of summer, especially if you stay near the ocean.

Stay out of the ocean at all times. This whole section runs to tide rips, sneaker waves that wash you off rocks, and other hazards to the unprepared. Instead, stop at the unobtrusive signs that indicate trails and other access to the many small creeks that cross Highway 1, and, of course, don't overlook the graceful arches of the bridge across the river that's probably appeared in more commercials than any other. Even with this, "commercial" doesn't apply to Big Sur—at least not yet!

For more information:
Chamber of Commerce, Big Sur, CA 93920.
District Ranger, Los Padres National Forest, 406 South Mildred, Kings City, CA 93930.

38.

Carmel Considered

As John Steinbeck noted, "If Carmel's founders should return they could not afford to live here . . . they would instantly be picked up as suspicious characters and deported over the city line." It's likely that in Steinbeck's 1940s and 1950s, locals moaned about the "good old 'seacoast of Bohemia' days" when authors and artists moved south out of the San Francisco Bay area to the beauty of the Coast before WWI.

Given the fact that it's a tidy little seaside town with a Hansel and Gretel atmosphere, narrow streets, and about five thousand residents. Bait the tourism hook with Clint Eastwood, and you have a challenge if you expect to enjoy the wonderful woods, lovely gardens, sprawling cypress trees, wide beaches, and the many moods of the Pacific. Admittedly the locals, at least many of them, make the tourist's life a bit easier these days with improved parking and such. However, their attitude toward changes is reflected in the requirement that you need a vote of the city council to remove a tree.

Unfortunately, most visitors stay in Monterey and drive into Carmel to jam the six square blocks of downtown for the day during summer. It's better to visit in other seasons. Monday of Thanksgiving week through Thanksgiving Day are the least crowded days of the year and massive discounts at the upscale shops deserve a look then. Try February when big storms pound the Coast—then you can zip from shop to shop and avoid the rain.

The basic approach to Carmel is simple—slip on sturdy shoes and walk! Park your vehicle where you stay in town, either at a nifty b and b or small hotel. Get up at first light to run or walk on the deserted beach, then head back, clean up, chow down, and check out shops and homes before the "drive-ins" arrive and, above all, don't even think about the car unless you're heading to out-of-town attractions such as Point Lobos or a drive past the plutocrats on 17-Mile Drive.

Breakfast very early or enjoy your b and b's included breakfast and graze around town. Try the pasta or sandwiches at Paolina's on San Carlos. Look around from 11:00 A.M. to 2:00 P.M., then enjoy an uncrowded late lunch. As an alternative, try the wonderful delis and pack lunch down to the beach. Explore side streets and the great gardens—locals are often friendly if you compliment their horticulture! Note the lack of sidewalks, and streetlights, and parking meters.

Carmel's odd approach to public amenities extends to few street numbers, no neon signs, and some oddly "Carmellian" diversions such as gas stations that look like British inns. Like the architecture, the art scene here offers rather too much "cute" for some tastes. If you like pedestrian seascapes in any genre, you're in luck. With nearly a hundred galleries, it takes a little time and a good eye to find the best values. At least you won't find T-shirt shops everywhere. You will find wonderful photography. The Weston Gallery at Sixth Avenue near Delores has winners—at a price.

Try dinner as soon as restaurants open; then it's a choice of varied night life or, if you've walked all day, a nice curl-up in front of a fireplace. It must be admitted that there are more than a fair share of neat pubs, coffeehouses, and other after-dinner attractions. Clint Eastwood, the one-time mayor, is a bigger attraction in town than the sea otters. So his Hog's Breath Inn gets a huge evening trade. His local fame may depend more on his push for the sale of ice cream by the scoop—ask the locals!—and his wonderful support for Tor House and other attractions than it does on his *Dirty Harry* doings.

During the middle of the day when the town loads up, head up into the Del Monte Forest towards Pacific Grove or check the paths through the flowers and redwoods in Mission Trail Park at Crespi and Mountain View. It's tough to get lost with the Pacific on one side and the bell tower of Mission San Carlos, Carmel's own, in view. The mission's still worth a tour in order to see the attached museum and to visit the grave of Father Serra, "father of the California missions."

Another nifty horticultural walk is rather shorter; it's the Biblical Gardens of the Church of the Wayfarer downtown off Seventh Avenue. There's every plant mentioned in the Bible here.

For more information:

Carmel Business Association, San Carlos and Seventh Avenue, Carmel-by-the-Sea, CA 93921, 408-624-2522 on weekdays.

Monterey Bay

39.

Monterey Wet

For old-timers, Monterey lost its way sometime between the closing of the canneries and the "flies in amber" paving of the historic section of Old Monterey—the Monterey of Richard Dana, John Steinbeck, and a host of forgotten fishermen. Today, the smell of caramel corn and the rumble of traffic replace the cannery stench locals called "the smell of money" and the cannery clanking. Some things are better. The Monterey Aquarium may be the best aquarium in the world, and may have been even before its 1996 expansion, and the Maritime Museum deserves a look.

However, it's not accidental that these two attractions look to the bay that made Monterey. Straying no more than a block or three from water is still the best recipe for a "Monterey Wet" weekend. Start with a stay on the bay at our favorite Monterey Bay Inn—leave the sliding doors open, and you can watch the bay and hills change color as the sun sets, and hear the gulls cry and seals roar. Hang over the rail here or the rail at Fisherman's Wharf and you'll see sea otters, too.

If you arrive in the afternoon, enjoy a walk past Cannery Row and the Monterey Aquarium to the shore delights of Pacific Grove and the historic Point Piños Lighthouse that's open from 1:00 to 4:00 P.M. for weekend tours. (See Pacific Grove, Chapter 40.)

Early in the morning, hike by the bay in the other direction to the historic district—sissies can drive and park by the wharf. The downtown Path of History offers crowds and confusion weekends and midday. But rise at dawn on a foggy summer or wet winter day, bundle up, and follow the Path through the fog. It's not hard to imagine ghosts of Richard Dana—do read *Two Years Before the Mast* for a look at old California. You can always come back to check our interiors later, yes?

Then head for what many locals call "the tourist pier." If you're very, very early, you might share coffee with anglers heading out to bottom fish for salmon or albacore. These half- and full-day trips offer quick access to the action and are highly recommended when the Pacific lives up to its name. Otherwise, you can catch small fish right off the pier or you might grab some fish scraps and stuff the pampered seals and sea lions who honk below the dock—they, too, profit from tourists. So do the fishmongers and wharf restaurants that offer delicious squid chowder by the cup or in a cannonball loaf of French bread along with fried squid, squid rings, and squid or crab salad and cocktails.

These take-out joys around the wharf present good fresh fish sans fuss or extra expense, and you should not miss sand dabs "on the bone" at least once a day. Tip: Only tourists opt for boneless fillets, and the waiter can pull the bones in a flash. It's a good thing sand dabs are too delicate to ship, otherwise they'd be as endangered as post-blackened redfish.

Other worthwhile Monterey munchies include hard-to-find local scampi, crabs from November until February, and just about anything on the Sardine Factory menu. Try the Sardine Factory for lunch, when you get dinner entrees without side dishes at savings. Another option worth the search is a deli picnic enjoyed on a pier or oceanside bench (buy stale bread for the gulls). Fortunately, there are enough Italians left in town to support delis. One of the best in town is just a couple of blocks from the Path of History.

However, when the tourists awake and pile into the parking lots, it's time to walk along the marina to Fisherman's Wharf #2, where the commercial anglers still land a massive squid catch that's replaced sardines in the local piscatorial economy. This is the pier to savor, the pier to sit on, the pier to fish, and the pier that retains its sense of worth and work. The Maritime Museum you pass isn't bad. It's not very big, does a decent job on local subjects, but seems rather a disappointment except to marine-history buffs. So check it out from the door and try it if you like it.

Then it's back to the room to rest feet before a visit to the world-class Monterey Aquarium that needs neither a tout nor much of a description. Its huge kelp tank, wonderful displays of often overlooked critters such as sea slugs and jellyfish, and the wonderful sea otters and shore displays deserve a morning and more. You even can watch a robot crawl along the bottom of Monterey Bay.

You might extend your aquatic pleasures onto or into the bay. During fall and winter, boats leave to watch the whales broach on their migrations. Birding trips are available, too, and you can book scenic cruises on both power and sail craft. Monterey Bay and Whaler's Cove at Point Lobos are wonderful diving sites if you don't mind sea otters messing with your regulator's bubbles. A host of dive shops along Lighthouse just inland from Cannery Row offer lessons, suits, and gear. Lighthouse offers all sports mountain-bike and roller-blade rentals. The paths along the shore cry out for self-propelled pleasures that give you the time to savor that special sense of surf, sand, and sun that's Monterey.

Stay near the bay, and you'll savor your stay!

For more information:

Monterey Peninsula Chamber of Commerce, Box 1770, Monterey, CA 93942-2198.

Monterey Bay Inn, 242 Cannery Row, Monterey, CA 93940, 800-424-6242.

40.

Pacific Grove

Since it hides its attractions between the tourist veneer of Monterey and the "if you have to ask you can't afford them" homes of Pebble Beach, Pacific Grove gets less respect than Rodney Dangerfield. That's too bad, for more than any other Monterey Peninsula city, Pacific Grove has retained its sense of place and past.

During the late 1800s, vacationing Methodists sought refreshing vacations and spiritual uplift at the Chautauqua Hall, and it's still there. This was sort of a combination of Billy Graham and a vaudeville show that filled time before movies and TV. You can make a case that the natural summer air conditioning—Monterey's fogs—were a major part of the attraction. When California's Central Valley cooks, the fogs are still nice and, more than anywhere else on the peninsula, Pacific Grove's the best spot to avoid crowds.

One of the ways to do this is by staying in a local b and b and, after a killer breakfast, "gazing and grazing" downtown along Lighthouse Avenue. Shops of various merit, ice cream, espresso, and an assortment of folks that might inhabit an old Fellini movie offer a moving feast for your eye and tummy and might take most of the afternoon. If your feet tire, buy a *Pine Cone* or other local paper, check out a bench, and watch the passing parade.

Old Pacific Grove stores, such as Holman's Department Store, survive in fact or in the memory of the money capsules that flashed on wires to the cashier's cage decades ago. New shops run to upscale clothing and whatever's politically correct in the edible line—except, of course, for some lethally rich Italian pastries and wonderful California sourdough breads and such.

If you must drive, start near Cannery Row and stay on your right on Ocean View along the water, where a host of tiny beaches run you around to the one-hundred-and-twenty-six-year-old Point Piños Lighthouse and on toward Asilomar Conference Center. The last is a sort of a transcendental-meditation, eat-veggies-and-explore-your-inner-self resort you expect to find in California. So there's usually something uplifting available, even though reservations are recommended at least a month ahead.

Frankly, I'd rather walk over or down from the day's digs and hike or bike along the curving bay-front road. Benches, a minibeach, and surf breaking on the mussel-decorated rocks make the day. Checking out tide pools and watching the water offer a sense of calm that's rare today.

If I must do something, I make sure my childhood favorite monarch butterflies have made it back to their "monarch tree." Then it's time to contemplate the dozens of restaurants that dot the peninsula. With luck, I can repeat this day with minor variations until it's time to head back to the confusion at home.

Classic Stays: The Centrella Hotel, built in 1889

just across the street from the above-mentioned Chautauqua Hall, offers a solid connection with this time period before Carmel was discovered by authors and photographers such as Jeffers and Steinbeck, Adams and Weston. It's now a nifty pink hotel with a couple of dozen rooms and five or so cottages, each with a fireplace, just three blocks from the ocean at Lovers' Point.

The bright yellow House of Seven Gables Inn's another antique classic with a "wonderview" of Monterey Bay. You also might consider the Gosby House Inn on Lighthouse Avenue, Pacific Grove's main street. All offer great breakfasts, and there's often an evening social hour with sherry and such.

For more information:

Centrella Hotel, 612 Central Avenue, Pacific Grove, CA 93950, 408-372-3372.

House of Seven Gables Inn, 555 Ocean View Boulevard, Pacific Grove, CA 93950, 408-372-4341.

Gosby House Inn, 641 Lighthouse Avenue, Pacific Grove, CA 93950, 408-375-1287.

41.

A Whale of a Weekend

California offers some of the best whale-watching in the world. Only Hawaii provides a better chance to see whales close up. Our namesake California grays once drew whalers to the Coast. These days, the massive mammals—large females reach fifty feet in length and top forty tons—now draw aquatic and shore-bound whale-watchers twice a year.

Migrations start in fall when whales, fattened on the krill and rich biomass of the Bering Sea, follow the Coast south for twelve thousand miles to Scammons and other Mexican lagoons where, in protected waters, they give birth to their young.

Nearly eighteen thousand of the twenty-two thousand grays in the world stay inshore of the California current to avoid killer whales and other predators as they closely approach traditional points and outlooks from the California border all the way to Mexico. These social creatures travel in small pods of two to six that swim close to the surface so they can be spotted by the white lace of their breathing, or "blows," as in "thar she blows," a whaler's call happily no longer heard in U.S. waters. It's not unknown to see other whale species, so you need to know that you can identify grays by their lack of dorsal fins.

Gray whales also breach, or leap out of the water, to either dislodge parasites from their thick hides or to let other whales know their position, depending on whom you believe. Even more interesting is "spyhopping," where a whale sticks its head out of the water in an almost vertical position. Some say this aids navigation; others claim whales use gravity to help swallow. Clearly there's a lot we don't know about whales!

We do know their migration dates. In the fall, watching starts early in December from Castle Rock near Crescent City and around Clam Beach and the headlands south of Ferndale. In Mendocino County, Mackerricher State Park near Fort Bragg offers good sightings from the beach. Perhaps the best point for landlubbers north of San Francisco is Point Reyes Lighthouse, where you can enjoy solid seminars on whales in January and February. Point Reyes Seminars (415-663-1200) offer just that.

Various San Francisco charter boats run whale trips to the Faralone Islands, but it's a shorter, quicker run out of Pilar Point Harbor or Monterey. If you like sailboats, look into Chardonnay Sailing Charters and its big catamaran out of Santa Cruz (408-423-1213). If you go out of San Francisco, check on Oceanic Society Expeditions out of Fort Mason (415-474-3385). Pismo and Avila Beach cruises fit nicely with weekends in San Luis Obispo or Morro Bay and might offer an extra attraction on a visit to San Simeon.

From Santa Barbara south, there are many options from December through April to catch herds migrating south and their return in March. Some of the best runs are out of Long Beach.

In San Diego, the Cabrillo National Whale-Watching Weekend in January offers speakers and a sheltered whale-watching station at Point Loma in San Diego, where locals watched Dennis Conner lose the America's Cup. It's a deal at $3 a car.

Dana Point offers its Festival of the Whales weekends in February through early March. There's a killer opening ceremony at La Plaza Park, a wonderful cruise-by, and moored inspections of tall ships at Dana Point Harbor, and the O.C Marine Instate has planned a fine exhibit, Whaling & Art of the Sailor. The last weekend of the festival features sand sculpture and whaling contests. (Information: 800-290-DANA.)

Mendocino's Whale Festival kicks in the first weekend in March with gallery exhibits and a massive pour of Mendocino wines. Check out the chowders and watch the whales from the headlands.

A couple of weeks later, in mid-March, Fort Bragg's Whale Festival switches to microbreweries. There's a short fun run and lots of whale-watching out of Noyo Harbor.

Weather makes a very large difference here. If it's windy and there are lots of whitecaps, unusual in

February or March, it's difficult to see whales blow, and you see fewer pods from ship or shore. Fortunately, all of the best whale-watching spots are wonderful weekend choices on their own. So if you miss out on the whales, you'll certainly find shopping, restaurants, and a host of other attractions.

42.

Literary Monterey—Steinbeck and Jeffers

In the thirty years that I've written travel pieces, I've doubtless had a hundred or more published on Monterey. Simply put: You should visit in winter, follow the Path of History, check the Maritime Museum, and spend a half day in the Aquarium. Take a whale-viewing boat tour in fall or spring and don't miss the sand dabs "on the bone" and the squid chowder on the wharf. Eat a lunch at the Sardine Factory.

With the usual tourist bits out of the way, let's look at a different Monterey Peninsula. Sometimes a bit of age connects you to a spot in a unique way. I increasingly feel that way about Monterey. Back in the early 1950s I read John Steinbeck's *Cannery Row* while sitting on a piling on the old wharf and waiting for mackerel to bite my line. I'd read Richard Dana's *Two Years Before the Mast*, a wonderful look at pre-Gold Rush California, even earlier.

Then two high-school friends and I met Mr. Steinbeck in Salinas and, from the goodness of a very great heart, he gave us permission to make a film of his wonderful short story, "Flight"—it still plays the art houses now and again.

I met Mr. Jeffers in the late 1960s at a school function. I didn't know what he did. I asked, and he told me "I'm a stonemason."

As I recall, my English teacher, a rather effete Eastern prep type, blanched and introduced me to "one of America's most distinguished poets." I was more impressed to meet the man who built the most wonderful house this side of Frank Lloyd Wright's Taliesin West. We ended up discussing "stone stacking."

Jeffers did a lot of that, and today his Tor House, with its Hawk's Tower, and poem deserve a long look, even though he's a bit out of favor as a poet:

"If you should look for this place after a handful of lifetimes;/Perhaps of my planted forest a few /May stand yet, dark-leaved Australians or the coast cypress,/ haggard/ With storm-drift; but fire and ax are devils."

Beginning in 1914, the small Tudor cottage, Tor House, and its Hawk's Tower were built by M.J. Murphy and a willing, and increasingly skilled, Jeffers with horse-dragged stones from the cove below. Jeffers had, as I remember it, some unpopular views about war.

Jeffers added stones from the Great Wall of China, lava from Mount Vesuvius, a porthole from the ship on which Napoleon fled Elba (and which sank off Monterey in 1830), and a host of other interesting bits and pieces. There's much, much more to see and explore in the house where Mr. Jeffers died in 1962 at age 75. Look for secret passages, tiny teapot-size fireplaces, and a Steinway piano built into the house.

The house is open from 10:00 A.M. to 3:00 P.M. on Fridays and Saturdays, and reservations are recommended for the hour-long tours that are limited to adults.

John Steinbeck's Monterey died with the closing of the canneries after WW II. Today, Monterey smells better, but it's far too full of tourists on big holiday weekends and summers for our tastes.

Steinbeck wouldn't have approved of today's sanitized Monterey. His *East of Eden* and *Cannery Row* offered a more basic look at mankind. This wasn't always appreciated when Steinbeck lived in Salinas and may have been one factor that led to his *Travels with Charlie*.

So to savor Steinbeck's Monterey start with a book—*Cannery Row* or *Tortilla Flats* for choice. Pick up a bottle of wine or some beer that Doc Ricketts would have liked. (Wonder what he would have thought of his lab being turned into an upscale private men's club?) Grab some sourdough bread or perhaps a cracked crab from a wharf fishmonger. Then check the weather. If it's foggy and you dress warmly, you're in luck. Try the Old Wharf—that's the one without all the restaurants. Find a spot where you share the rail with anglers on the side away from the yuppie fishing boats. Then, if you squint a bit, you can imagine old Monterey as the foghorns honk, seals bleat, and the gulls cry. Read a few pages. Drink a bit. Eat a bit. Sooner than you think, you'll be straining to see the last pages as the light fades. Then close your eyes and listen, and you'll hear Steinbeck's Monterey. Finally, check out Steinbeck's Salinas on your way home (see Steinbeck's Salinas in Chapter 47).

For more information:

Tor House Foundation, 408-624-1813.

43.

Santa Cruz Beaches

Old-time amusement-park roller coasters used to loom above beach towns from San Francisco to San Diego in the happy days when life itself was a beach. Today, save for the Santa Monica Pier and such, only the State Historical Landmark Santa Cruz's Beach and Boardwalk remains. Like the Municipal Wharf, it's a good place to visit on any Santa Cruz weekend. Granted, Santa Cruz has the cultural attractions of a major university, weather that's as good as Monterey's, and far too many other offerings to even list. However, beaches and boardwalks make beach towns, and Santa Cruz has far more than its share.

Consider Natural Bridges Beach and its bridges and incredible tide pools. Then there's Cowell Beach with its Club Ed sailboarding and surfing lessons. Or Santa Cruz Beach with its wide sand, decent swimming, and the multitude of Muni Pier attractions such as the Stagnaro boats that pack anglers in on weekends and the markets and restaurants that feature—what else?—fish. There's even some parking.

The Boardwalk just behind the beach retains its 1950s' flavor with classic games such as skee ball, a killer 1924 Giant Dipper roller coaster, and enough other rides to cause even the most gung-ho teens to upchuck their cotton candy. Small fry and smart adults should try the 1911 Looff Carousel and its hand-carved animals. Both rides are National Historic Landmarks. Neptune's Kingdom in the 1907 Plunge Building runs to miniature golf courses, talking pirates, and enough games to keep kids off the beach on rainy days. "Mature" big-band addicts might remember the Coconut Grove that today offers Sunday brunch and, from time to time, big bands.

Seasonal Boardwalk attractions include a February Clam Chowder Cook-off and the Ultimate Pasta Cook-off. If you're athletically inclined, you can try the Sprout Toss or Sprout Putt during the Brussels Sprout Festival.

The south end of the Boardwalk's a short cast from the San Lorenzo River and from San Lorenzo Park with its bowling green and picnic site. Once-massive steelhead runs in the river are hanging on with considerable help.

Downtown Santa Cruz has recovered from the last earthquake nicely and suits pedestrians and bike riders best. "Berkeley on the Bay" describes it best. Mission Santa Cruz, an 1856 replica of the 1794 original, doesn't seem as interesting as the many wildly painted Victorian homes or even Casa Adobe, the oldest building in town.

The Pacific Avenue Mall shows what shopping should be like in beach towns. If your tastes runs to this, the Mission-style Civic Auditorium is the site of the Miss California Pageant, and the Chamber of Commerce here has bags of material on Santa Cruz attractions. It's also wise to check on University of California Santa Cruz offerings such as affordable concerts. The campus on the hills overlooking town deserves at least a drive through.

Twin Lakes Beach, south of Santa Cruz, sports its own state park and the usual beach attractions; it's a nice place to picnic. Don't overlook the chance to sail. You can take lessons, sail on the *Chardonnay II,* try a high-speed catamaran, or charter a schooner. Whale-watching is a treat (see Chapter 41), and if you have a body to dispose of, there are burials at sea.

Capitola Beach offers good diving, decent fishing, and the odd clam the sea otters missed. The Antonelli Begonia Gardens in Capitola offer a free look at wonderful begonias that do well along the foggy coast; blooms peak from August to November. If you garden, this can be expensive, as they sell wonderful plants.

New Brighton Beach State Park, south of Capitola, gets our vote as a best bet for campers. It's open all year and, like Santa Cruz, seems a wonderful choice for winter camping and not a bad choice for summer visitors from California hot spots such as Sacramento.

Seacliff, Manresa, and Sunset beaches follow the curve of Monterey Bay down past Watsonville that's best known for its garlic festival. Stay on Highway 1 and you'll sample the best of a section of the Coast that most miss in their haste to head for the Monterey Peninsula on Highway 101. Stock up on artichokes in Castroville before you head home.

For more information:

Santa Cruz County Conference & Visitors Council, 701 Front Street, Santa Cruz, CA 95060, 408-425-1234.

Santa Cruz Boardwalk, 400 Beach Street, Santa Cruz, CA 95060-5491.

O'Neil Yachts, 2222 East Cliff Drive, Santa Cruz, CA 95062, 408-476-5200.

Boardwalk, 408-426-7433.

Chardonnay II Cruises, 408-423-1213.

Club Ed Surf and Windsurf School, Cowell Beach in front of the Dream Inn,

800-287-SURF or 408-459-WAVE.

Inland

44.

Peninsula Pleasures

If you've ever tried to head over the bridge between Martinez and Benicia or into the Monterey Peninsula from Highway 101 on a Friday, you might suspect that there's a rule you must drive at least two hundred miles from home to find a wonderful weekend. Fortunately, such isn't the case. In middle California, for example, the San Francisco Peninsula and San Jose residents have thousands of acres of redwoods, tons of red wine, bountiful beaches and bays, and enough camping and coddling at b and bs to suit anyone.

All this hides in the hills less than an hour from San Mateo or San Jose. It doesn't take much longer for East Bay residents to enjoy the Peninsula action, either, as you'll whiz against traffic on the Dumbarton Bridge any Friday night.

Fall and spring offer the best times to visit, with wine harvests and pumpkin patches and wildflowers and green hills, respectively. A host of pleasantly winding roads network the mountains and exploring new roads brings its own rewards in artists' studios, farms—organic and otherwise—and splendid vistas of the Pacific.

However, it's important that you avoid the check-list approach. Take your time, take a lunch, take a book, stop if something looks interesting. Save something for next trip. You've San Francisco Bay on one side and the Pacific Ocean on the other, so you can't get lost.

For starters, the Santa Cruz Mountains offer wonderful redwoods in a belt that runs from Big

Basin State Park in the north down through Henry Cowell Redwoods State Park a nice spot to picnic, camp, trout fish, barbecue, or hike. Crest hiking trails are particularly attractive on summer days when San Jose fries and the cooling coast fogs that water the redwoods march up the west slopes and spill across the crest.

There's no better place to bike! You can coast out the day from the crest to the Pacific as your shuttle-car driver munches croissants in Santa Cruz before hitting the shops. Like to drive? Two-lane roads through the redwoods—given an absence of RVs—offer chances. If you ride, a host of horseback trips are available. Then there are scenic flights for an overview, or you can fly kites, that most relaxing of pastimes! There are spots on the crest where, during March, you could fly lawn chairs.

You do have to get there. The quick and dirty route is Highway 17 to Santa Cruz through Scotts Valley and Santa's Village—don't ask! It isn't bad very early on Saturday, but try the Mount Herman cutoff to Felton and Highway 9 before you get to Santa Cruz.

Felton offers the nifty Roaring Camp & Big Trees narrow-gauge railroad rides during spring, summer, and fall. There's a tooting excursion, the "Suntan Special," to Santa Cruz beaches. It leaves Roaring Camp early in the morning, goes down the canyon of the San Lorenzo, over wood bridges, and, once in town, past Victorian buildings. Afternoon return trips limit shuttle cars. There's another trip up the mountain for picnicking, a chuck-wagon barbecue on weekends, and a collection of seasonal attractions such as Mountain Men's Roundevous.

You also could take Graham Hill Road down to Santa Cruz instead of Highway 9 (See Chapter 43 on Santa Cruz) or follow Felton Empire Road to

Bonny Doon Road and go on down to Highway 1 past special attractions such as the Bonny Doon Vineyard. Then either head north up Highway 1 and cut back across the mountains, or return to Highway 9 and follow it toward San Mateo as your fancy directs.

Cabernets or chardonnays from Bonny Doon, Soquel's Bargettos, or Felton's Hallcrest vineyards go nicely with seasonal fresh produce from the farm trails. You can even buy Thanksgiving pumpkins or cut Christmas trees. You'll find ceramics, wood carvings, paintings, weather vanes, and much else. Off-spots, such as Weatherly Castle in Ben Lomond, sprout like mushrooms after a rain all over the Santa Cruz Mountains. Then, when you run out of time, chug down Highway 9 or 17 to the Freeway and zip home.

If you want to stay overnight and this makes for a more relaxing weekend, camp at Cowell or Big Basin State Parks or consider Santa Cruz urban or mountain b and bs. As one local notes, "The hills are alive with the sound of pesto pounding," so there's a host of decent restaurants, small inns, and other eateries. It's a trip, and a wonderfully accessible one.

For more information:
Check with the Santa Cruz Visitor's and Convention Bureau, 800-833-3494.
For a winery list and map: 408-479-Wine.
For artists studios: 800-833-3494.

45.

The South Delta

The Sacramento River and the North Delta or the West Delta complex of resorts, houseboat rentals, and waterways attract ninety percent of delta visitors. The scenic South Delta in and around the San Joaquin, Middle, and Old Rivers, with sloughs, waterways, the Grant Line Canal, and other backwaters worth the exploration, gets the smart delta visitors who enjoy the least-known section of the massive thousand-square-mile Delta Country. (See Delta North, Chapter 73, and Sacramento Locomotion, Chapter 71, in the North California section.)

Perhaps the Silicon Valley folks' smarts extends to more than computers, for a large percentage of the acceptable number of South Delta visitors come from San Jose and other South Bay residents. It's not hard to head over through Livermore and Tracy, either.

Best of all, there's not much to do here if you're not aquatic. The banks run to farmland, and cuts and canals are often separated from levee-top roads by considerable masses of cattails and blackberry patches big enough for all the rabbits in Australia. So access to the water is limited to resorts and open or riprap bank areas. Fortunately, there's a wide range of resorts.

Discovery Bay, at the upper end of the scale with about three thousand homes either on the water or a golf course, does offer all the amenities anyone needs, and kids like the water slides at Oakwood Lake Resort. But the best way to visit is a weekend houseboat rental (see above) that lets you putt along back canals and cuts and check out the crawdad collecting and catfish action. The South Delta is also a solid choice for black bass, panfish, and, in season, shad and other species such as stripers, salmon, or sturgeon.

Rent a houseboat in Stockton at the Village West Marina, largest in the delta, and you can chug down Grant Line Canal, Old River, and the San Joaquin or head back into a host of canals that run south toward Tracy. You'll find this end far less windy than the West Delta and much less crowded than the waters north of the San Joaquin. Less wind makes this a great spot to water ski—rental boats and gear available—as the water warms faster than in the rivers in the back canals. Given calm waters, it's rather odd that Stockton sports the largest inland sailing club west of the Mississippi—whoever said "rag baggers" made sense.

Stockton also offers the chance to take advantage of cross wakes from oceangoing freighters; you may have the right of way, but it takes a mile or so for freighters to stop, and they can't leave the dredges channel, so watch out! Stockton's also a dandy spot for seasonal attractions such as boat shows and, of course, one of the best fireworks exhibits anywhere has been put on for decades by Baron Hilton at the Mandeville Tip. The lighted-boat Christmas parade's a nice choice, too.

Seasonal visits each offer their own pleasures. Winter finds a lot of attractions closed, and fog sometimes is a problem in exchange for a water-wilderness experience. Spring greens up the shore, improves the fishing, and if you don't get massive Sierra runoffs to muddy the waters, is a prime time to visit.

Summer suits the swimsuit and waterski set who like hot weather and the wild assortment of food and services at the incredible collection of smaller marinas and shops on South Delta backwaters.

Fall may be the best of all seasons. It's quite safe

even with the odd shotgun hunter out for ducks or pheasants. The waters stay calm until winter storms, and you can add in all sorts of fruit trails and produce stands going or coming. Fall's also a good time to visit by car if you don't mind sharing levee roads with trucks full of produce.

The easy way to drive the delta is on laterals in from Interstate 5. The hard way to drive is away from the delta after a quiet weekend.

For more information:

California Delta Chambers, Box 177, 49 Main Street, Isleton, CA 95641, 916-777-5007.

46.

Life Before Interstate 5

Interstates, like jet aircraft, get you there fast but without much of a sense of place. You see the same gas stations, quick stops, KOAs, and chain motels all over America. However, if you get off onto the old roads, the roads with history that run through the main streets of small towns, past fruit stands, and, if you're lucky, to old-time cafes, where locals discuss who's doing what with whom, and if you seem reasonable, can fill you in on the best local attractions. More than any other in California, Highway 99 gives you a sense of the state's agricultural base. Drive it one way and then take Interstate 5 or the slower but more scenic Highway 101 home along the coast, and you've a classic California car tour that crosses most Sierra rivers in their tame lower ends.

In the "good old days," Highway 99 took Californians from Mexicali, Mexico, up the east side of the Great Central Valley through agricultural centers like Fresno to Sacramento long before

Interstate 5 replaced Highway 101 as the main north-south route between Los Angeles and San Francisco. Old 99 springs away from Interstate 5 at the Tejon oil fields and bisects Bakersfield before it heads through the agricultural towns to Delano, Turlare, Fresno, and Stockton before it hits Sacramento.

Bakersfield, a mining town back in 1885, now runs to cotton, alfalfa, fruit, and what's left of the California oil business. It's a typical valley town on a river, and it's a good spot from which to head up into the Sierras and the Kern River Canyon via Highway 178 .

Agriculture flourishes all the way up to Fresno, "the world's raisin center" and a source of grapes for affordable wines. Check out the raisin plants and get off onto back roads for summer fruit stands. The tour of the local Sun Maid plant will teach you more than anyone wants to know about raisins.

Literary folks find nearby Hanford and the historic 1880 fight at Mussel Slough between ranchers and the railroad folks of interest, as it prompted Frank Norris's *The Octopus,* a wonderful whistle-blowing book. Head east and you're in Sequoia and Kings Canyon. (See the Central Sierra and Fun in the Foothill sections).

Fortunately, it's easy to turn off Highway 99, known as Old 99. Most laterals to the east reach up into the foothills for spring flowers. Oddly enough, we prefer winter when the land is serene and dark to spring when the fields burst into green, but each season has its own pleasures—even hot and dusty summer. Fall's nice if you don't mind sharing the road with big trucks packed with produce.

Agriculture does offer rewards. You'll spot, and can sample, the fruits of fig, pear, peach, plum, and other trees, as well as date palms and more. Stop, check out the harvests, ask questions, and meet the locals. You'll get an idea of agriculture. Such trips, given a decent back seat and housebroken kids, offer an education worth the time. California's agriculture hasn't entirely disappeared under parking lots and highways.

47.

Salinas, "Seca," Steinbeck, and Super Cars

Interstate 5 gets you there faster. Highway 1 is the scenic choice if you drive north so you're on the inside, but Highway 101 seems the most sensible north-south route in California. Salinas may be the city on Highway 101 that gets the least tourism, and that's a shame, for it offers the agricultural splendors of the Central Valley, a tiny drive from the Monterey Peninsula. Tip: Folks on a budget stay in Salinas for less. There's dandy inexpensive Mexican food here, too.

Salinas does have a couple of major attractions: a rodeo and an author. The California State Rodeo is huge, crowded, and a high spot for those whose pleasures run to broncos, bullriding, cowboy hats, and the pickup set. Frankly, this seems to work best for the country folks who don't mind sweating out a day of dust.

Oddly enough, Salinas now considers John Steinbeck to be its favorite son. They named the city library on 110 West Luis Street after him and have wonderful exhibits on, and some recordings of, him. There's even an East of Eden restaurant in a local church. Note: It's probable that, with apologies to James Dean, both *Sweet Thursday* and *Cannery Row* were better books.

You also can enjoy a modest lunch at the

restaurant and a tour of the house described in *East of Eden* as "It was an immaculate and friendly house, grand enough, but not pretentious, and it sat inside its white fence surrounded by clipped lawn. . . ."

What makes this rather odd is Steinbeck's reception in Salinas after his novels and short stories. Supposedly, the favorite game in town was guessing which character related to whom and which house was which. City fathers didn't exactly jump for joy at his characters, who sometimes sported with ladies of rental virtue, and the respectables in town who took their high jinks to Monterey. It's rumored that some divorces followed the book, and that his *Travels with Charlie* resulted from, among other things, difficulties with locals. Now, of course, he's politically correct.

If you visit Salinas or Monterey in late August, you've another option—the annual Monterey Historic Automobile Races that usually run along with the Pebble Beach Concours d'Elegance. The curving, winding up and down one and nine-tenths miles of Laguna Seca Race is just off Highway 68, the back road between Monterey and Salinas. Granted this crowds the Peninsula, but it's a wonderful attraction to car buffs.

This kind of racing's rather informal, as the cars and drivers aren't spring chickens, and both are worth too much to risk. Spectators perch where they like. Try the inside of bends and stay out of range of stray vehicles. You need to get there early, spread a cloth, and enjoy a picnic lunch, unless you're one of the sissies who opt for the grandstand.

Most years, the gates open at 7:00 A.M.; warm-ups run from 9:00 A.M. to noon, and racing starts after lunch and goes until about 4:30 P.M. Different classes run: racing cars from 1910 to 1947, sports race cars from 1948 to 1962, and GT racing cars from 1948 to 1966. It's wise to order tickets and arrive early so you can stroll through the paddocks and check out the cars.

Then, after the noise and confusion of race day, enjoy the peninsula before you head for the lawn of the Lodge at Pebble Beach (Del Monte Lodge to longtime locals). Then it's time to head for home. Oh, well, at least your car's paid for!

For more information:

Salinas Visitors and Convention Bureau, Box 1170, Salinas, CA 93902.

48.

The Land Railroads Made

It's fourteen thousand miles around Cape Horn, three months via the Panama Canal, seventeen days by stage, or eight days by Pony Express if you're a letter. Only after the Central Pacific Railroad from Sacramento and the Union Pacific from Missouri ended their great race in Promontory Summit, Utah, was California really part of the Union. Later, rails and refrigerated cars sent California produce eastward. The Southern Pacific route from New Orleans to Los Angeles connected the southland. Other links, such as the Daylight, laced the West Coast and Central Valley. The Atchison, Topeka & Santa Fe Railroad, the Union Pacific RR made California a rail state (and, it might be added, led to abuses as noted in Frank Norris's fine book, *The Octopus*).

One way to understand the importance of railroads is with a visit to Sacramento's magnificent rail museum (see Chapter 71 on Sacramento). Other ways once included trips through the Feather River

Canyon, but these days you're rather more limited. One option would be a trip on the California *Zephyr* that runs from Oakland to Chicago up and over the Donner Pass. Get off in Reno, enjoy Saturday night, and return the following morning.

The *Coast Starlight* from Los Angeles to Seattle offers a dandy coast route to San Francisco for an overnight and a return the next day. And, if you're a rabid rail buff, a number of other options present, past, and mostly threatened offer additional weekend outings, such as the *Southwest Chief* from Los Angeles to Chicago or the *San Joaquin* from Oakland to Bakersfield in the Central Valley or the *San Diegans* from Santa Barbara to San Diego. If you need not ask the cost, you can even opt for private cars, which are rented through the American Association of Private Railroad Car Owners, on any Amtrak route.

However, most of the fun's on short trips that exactly suit weekends. Theme-park trains in Knotts Berry Farm, Great America, or the Disneyland Railroad and Monorail offer rides that aren't exactly authentic but suit kids.

Rail buffs prefer either working modern options such as the San Diego Trolley, San Jose metro, and vintage streetcars on the loop at the downtown transit mall. Then there's Sacramento's RT Metro, which mixes freeway median and downtown streets, or the Mini Metro system in San Francisco. BART, which tunnels under San Francisco Bay, offers another modern system worth a ride.

Traditional options include San Francisco's trolley cars (don't miss the museum), or longer rides on steamers such as *Railtown* 1897 or the *Santa Cruz Roaring Camp and Big Trees* or the *Skunk* and *Super Skunk* between Willits and Fort Bragg. Electrics from the Bay Area trolley lines and the Sacramento

Northern Railroad still run at the Western Railway Museum near Fairfield.

However, there's a big difference between riding a train and driving a train. For $75 an hour, you can run a diesel Alco Western Pacific engine. This is an incredible treat and quite affordable if split among four. You can each take a turn with one hand on the brake and one on the throttle.

If posh suits, the Napa Valley Wine Train runs fifteen trains a week from Napa to St. Helena for lunch or dinner. You don't move very fast and you see the backs of a lot of homes, but the mid- to long-range views of the Napa Valley offer a decent evening and, for most, a chance to dress up a bit.

At the other end of the fiscal scale, there's the Niles Canyon Railroad that runs a couple of free trips on four miles of Niles Canyon rails that were once part of the Transcontinental Railroad.

Keep an eye out as you enjoy the weekend, and you'll find lots more rail options that give you an idea of the one-time importance of train travel. Next time you're stuck on Interstate 80 in Sacramento or watch the BART trains whipping past on the Bayshore or are getting passed by the Tijuana Trolley, think about rails. They're coming back. There's even a high-speed train like those in France or Japan projected to connect L.A. to Las Vegas.

For more information:
Amtrak, 800-USA-RAIL.
Niles Canyon Railroad, 510-462-4557.
Portola Railroad Museum, 916-832-4141.

Fun in the Foothills

49.

Highway 49 South

Highway 49, as you might expect from the name, runs through 49er country from the southernmost diggings around Oakhurst, all the way along the foothill mining town of the Gold Country and Northern Mines, to its terminus on Highway 70 not far from Hallelujah Junction, a half hour north and west of Reno.

It's impossible to cover Highway 49 in a weekend, and its nine counties have features enough to justify an entire summer's weekends if you add in all the hiking, fishing, biking, and boating. So we had the gall to concentrate on the historic towns, after we divided the Gold Country into two parts with the five southern counties here and the four northern counties in the Northern California section. Do realize that from anywhere on Highway 49 you're never more than a half hour from the High Sierra lodgepoles or from a major foothill reservoir with boats, houseboats, and more.

It's important to know that the Gold Country grew from the "Mother Lode," the band of quartz along the foothills west of the massive blocks of the Sierra's granite. This held all the gold that worked up from the primal deeps along cracks in the frangible quartz. Eons of erosion ground quartz to sand and moved heavy gold to the bottom of streams present or past. Stream, or placer, gold got things going at Coloma and named Placer County, but the real riches came from quartz veins worked in large part by Welsh and other skilled hard-rock miners with heavy equipment.

Given this, let's look at the five southern counties: Madera, Mariposa, Tuolumne, Calaveras, and Amador. Even the names are interesting. Tuolumne is Mi-Wok Indian for "stone house." The rest come from the Spanish and mean, respectively, "lumber," "butterfly," "skulls," and "love of gold."

Madera County: Check out Yosemite's Southern Mines, where gold was discovered in 1850. Check the Ahwahnee flume built by the Sugar Pine Lumber Company that watered Madera.

Mariposa: Mariposa's now the usual gateway to Yosemite National Park through its El Portal entrance. It offers a few historic buildings, the oldest courthouse in California in continuous use, the *Gazette* newspaper office and, at Mount Bullion, the remains of the Princeton Mine. Nearby spots like Coulterville with its interesting mining locomotive and hangman's tree or Mormon Bar deserve a look. You even can find the ruins of the Ghiradelli Store, built when Ghiradelli Square in San Francisco was but a glimmer of hope.

Tuolumne County: Sonora, the county seat, and Columbia, the most lovingly restored of the Mother Lode cities, deserve chapters of their own. Columbia State Historic Park once had a population of fifteen thousand and produced $87 million worth of gold—and this at $35 an ounce. It's well-preserved with decent restaurants, wood sidewalks, gold panning, shops, museums, candy stores, and lots more. It's wonderful if you're there before the shops open and the crowds arrive; it grows less attractive in the middle of the day when smart visitors are down on the Stanislaus River rafting or swimming up at Pinecrest. There's some dandy rafting, too.

Big Oak Flat Roads, a good northern entrance to Yosemite, and the Railtown and Sierra Railroad offer solid tours and trips, and the Railtown, 1897, State Park offers steam train rides. You're in Mark Twain and Bret Harte country here, and the area's become a favorite with burned-out urban types who have opened more b and bs than you might expect. Get a county guide and drop in as you drive or walk by.

Calaveras County: Frogs jump here where once a hundred-and-sixty-pound gold nugget, the second largest ever, came out of Carson Hill in 1854. But the gold for today's visitor is literary and amphibian. Stories like "Jumping Frog of Calaveras" or the "Outcasts of Poker Flat" suggest a brush-up on your Bret Harte or Mark Twain. I'd stay out of town during the Frog Jump Jubilee on the third weekend in May, but Angles Camp deserves a good look otherwise.

Mercer Caverns, just a bit off Highway 49 in Murphy, offers a cool break on hot summer days. General Ulysses S. Grant stayed at Murphy's Hotel, which still has historic suites, a decent restaurant, and reasonable rates. Nice ice cream at the stand in town, too.

It's not far past Murphy's to the Calaveras Big Trees State Park, which is particularly attractive in winter with a light dusting of snow to replace summer's light coating of dust. Up and over Ebbets Pass gets you to snow country, trout fishing, and more.

Amador County: Jackson, the county seat, gets most of the action with a decent county museum that has better-than-average mining models, but the D'Agostini Winery is a nice summer or fall stop.

Amador City bills itself as the smallest incorporated city in the US, but the most wonderful town on Highway 49 may be Sutter Creek. It takes at least a day to explore all the historic buildings on Main Street and the even more interesting homes off Main that most tourists miss. The Knight Foundry is the only working water-powered foundry in the US. Nice wrought iron and more at the foundry, and much, much more at the many antiques shops here. There's a fine choice of restaurants, b and bs, and a neat old hotel.

Head up and over Highway 88, the southernmost of the all-year Sierra crossings, and you drive past some dandy trout streams and lakes, and then you're in Kirkwood Ski Area and Tahoe. There's good walk-in fishing, excellent hiking trails, and a host of resorts. Fine country, and it's a quick trip from Sacramento or Highway 5 for most.

For more information:
The Golden Chain Council of the Mother Lode, Inc., Box 7046, Auburn, CA 95604.

50.

Reliable Reservoirs

Sierra rivers used to flood the Great Central Valley of California on almost a yearly basis. Today, a massive series of Sierra and low foothill impoundments water agricultural lands, fill swimming pools, and provide drinking water. In exchange for this, and with it the drowning of some rivers, reservoirs offer a wonderful selection of aquatic options all year. However, wise visitors think spring when the water's up, the wildflowers are fresh, and the grass is green, even though higher-elevation waters may still be snowbound.

From south to north, you'll find McLure, and Don Pedro, on both sides of Highway 49, then Hogan/New Hogan Reservoir, Camanche, New Melones and Tulloch Reservoirs, Lake Amador, Pardee Lake, and in the north, Folsom Reservoir. These are just the best-known "starters." Note: Skip the last one except for day trips or off-season visits out of the state capital, since it's always mobbed in the summer.

Most of these offer shore camping. If you own, borrow, or rent a boat, you can find a piece of shore to temporarily call your own. Of if you like, try a comfortable houseboat or a reasonably priced resort.

All of these waters offer fishing, most feature resorts, marinas, and shore camping, and rental houseboats, skiffs, or ski boats increase your options. Tip: combine dawn or dusk reservoir visits with a Highway 49 or Central Valley drive during the heat of the day, and you can catch more fish and scout the waters that might suit you best on a return visit.

To help you search, here's a thumbnail sketch of each spot. Unless otherwise noted, you'll find camping, fishing, a marina, picnicking, and more. You'll also find that water levels, marina services, and campgrounds seem to vary from year to year. So scout before you invest a precious weekend.

Hogan Reservoir—new Hogan Reservoir buried old Hogan; and the submerged dam is a good fishing choice. This four-thousand-acre reservoir has wonderful boaters'-only campgrounds and some spiffy fall or spring striped-bass fishing before or after the water skiers go through.

Camanche Lake has major resort developments and wide ramps on both north and south shores of its nearly eight thousand acres. It's one of the best-known lakes in California, with a mix of bass, trout,

Minimalist reservoir fishing

crappie, and other species. During summer, try night fishing for crappie or catfish. If fishing pales, it is not far to the pleasures of Mokelumne Hill or Jackson.

Lake Amador and *Pardee Lake* are less than fifty miles from Stockton and are particularly well suited to those who fish or paddle since there's neither waterskiing nor jet-skiing, and coves on both lakes offer protected waters. Pardee's a good choice for trout; Amador adds bass.

New Melones combines nicely with a visit to Columbia or Sonora. It's a huge lake and sometimes windy, so it's not our first summertime choice. We prefer *Tulloch Reservoir* downstream, which is shaded nicely in deep canyons for cruising.

Don Pedro is the Los Angeles of Central California waters, as it covers thirteen thousand acres and holds trout, bass, landlocked salmon, and much else. There are too many marinas to count. If you like big water and don't mind sharing it, this is a good spot to fish. We prefer the side north of Highway 49.

All of these reservoirs, and a host of others, are covered in Tom Steinstra's *The Complete Guide to California Fishing.* This highly recommended book rates all waters from one to ten and is updated every year or two. It is an absolute must for anglers.

Since God no longer makes streams, but reservoirs continue to thrive, you might as well go where the flow stops and check a reliable reservoir you can visit often even if you don't fish.

51.

Why Not White Water?

White water comes in more California flavors than Baskin & Robbins ice cream. You can paddle inflatable rubber duckies down easy Klamath River riffles; you can paddle a raft while perched on the tube or grab ropes as your guide rows through bigger water; you might try tough runs on rivers such as the Upper Tuolumne.

Rivers rate from canoeable and "mostly" Class One, such as the American River from Nimbus Dam to Discovery Park on the Sacramento River, up to Class Five, offering an interesting chance to risk life and limb. Trips run from a half-day on the American River below Nimbus up to two or three days or more on larger, more interesting wilderness waters such as the Tuolumne "T" Rivers. There are White Water Schools to teach skills, too.

These days, regulations limit trips to a few a day so you can enjoy isolation and the essence of a river experience on rivers such as the T, a gem with a steep gradient, and lovely long rapids, such as Nemesis, The Squeeze, Gray's Grindstone, and the infamous Clavey Falls (this has an optional footpath for the less adventurous). Add sandy beaches, old Mi-wok Indian and more recent Gold Rush ruins, deer, and other wildlife. Compound the pleasures of the day with deep canyons that have pools for swimming, and you've answered the question "Why not white water?"

There are other rivers worth running besides the T. In Southern California, the Kings River offers easy water. The Stanislaus and the Class Five rafter's favorite, the North Fork of the American, deserve a try after skills build.

An assortment of outfitters—all must be both licensed and insured—offer trips, and you need to reserve early for a place on the wilderness waters during the prime spring runoff. You'll need to opt for either a paddle or oar raft. In the former, you perch on the tub, get yelled at a lot, and develop interesting aches at the end of a paddle day—great fun for the sedentary! Oar rafts put you at your ease if you ignore white knuckles and don't believe all of the guide's war stories.

Costs seem reasonable if you consider they include food and lodging, and there's no shopping along the river. As a rule, you pay a deposit of $100 or so and must pay sixty days in advance of the trip. You may, in some years, find trips canceled due to wild water or major storms, but you get a full refund.

Come as you are. Basic gear does the job as the outfitter includes waterproof bags, meals, shuttle services, and other things you need. You might want to rent sleeping bags, tents, or early and late in the year, wet suits. Some firms even take videos so you can amaze your friends later! All firms provide waterproof containers for cameras if you take your own photos. Be honest about your physical condition and fear level, and you'll get put on the right trip.

For more information:

Sierra Mac River Trips, Box 366, Sonora, CA 95370, 800-457-2580.

52.

Highway 41—More Than Yosemite

It's easy to zip up Highway 41 from Southern California to Yosemite; it's also a bit dim in summer unless you really like Yosemite crowds. So rather than rushing, take it easy, leave the highway, drive country lanes, and check out local attractions in oddly named towns like Coarsegold and Fish Camp. Do consider Bass Lake (see Chapter 53 on Bass Lake) and, if you have a longer vacation, consider three or four days. Highway 41 traverses the most historic foothill towns in Southern Mines, Gold Country, and Northern Mines past Tahoe.

Fresno deserves a look on its own if only for its wonderful Armenian food, but it's upward and onward through the foothill oaks into Coarsegold where fifteen hundred gold miners panned local creeks. As usual in the Gold Country, the real money came out of a hard-rock mine called Texas Flats. The Coarsegold Inn features some dandy weekend concerts, solid but not fancy food, and a nearby market that's a good spot to pick up picnic makings.

If you expect decent motel accommodations or can't get Yosemite reservations, Oakhurst offers a solid selection at the south end of the three hundred and ten miles of Highway 49, perhaps the most scenic backroad in California. It's only fifteen miles to the south entrance of Yosemite.

It's easy to overlook options such as golf at the Ahwahnee Resort and Country Club, the hayrides and Doc Holliday's "Bar-B-Que" at Sierra Sky Ranch Resort, and a host of pleasures for hikers, horseback riders, water skiers, and others.

Old Town, at the south end of the city, offers its own Boot Hill, a logger's choice of historic buildings, and the other attractions of "Fresno Flats" as Oakhurst was called in the old days when city fathers accepted names like "Hangtown." If you're a history buff, consider the local bookstores, which offer a wonderful collection of tales about the foothills and Sierra.

And check Fresno Flats' Historic Park's restored homes. One, built in 1869 and moved to the present site, features massive sugar-pine logs that once carpeted the Sierras' intermediate elevations. Sugar pines are easy to spot with their huge, long pine cones. The museum at the park, the blacksmith shop, and other exhibits aren't quite as flossy as you'll find in Columbia near Sonora, but the area's considerably less crowded. The park is open Wednesday through Sunday.

Check on seasonal attractions such as the Mountain Peddlers' Antiques and Collectors' Flea Market and Craft Fair. These usually run on Memorial and Labor Day weekends and offer more food than anyone can eat (try the Indian tacos) and more antiques than anyone could buy (some do try). The May Balloon Festival that launches a hundred or more balloons from the Madera Airport also deserves a look.

However, our favorite Oakhurst attraction is the Golden Chain Theater which runs to summer melodramas in a converted bowling alley. Frankly, while the melodramas are fun, we prefer the fall and Christmas performances.

Fish Camp: Toward Yosemite's entrance, Fish Camp, aside from the suggestive name, offers the Yosemite Mountain Sugar Pine Railroad. This runs steam-powered Shay engines and Model-A powered rail cars popular on historic logging railroads four miles up into national-forest land with decent views of the Nelder Grove of giant redwoods. The peak in the background is Mount Raymond.

Shays, built between 1880 and 1945, are the Jeeps of railroad engines as each of their wheels is a driving wheel and articulated so that with the short wheelbase, they can handle both steep and curved tracks with gusto. This is, unfortunately, a mostly summer attraction, running from April to November with the rail cars and from July to September with the Shays.

If you visit during summer, pick up picnic makings in Oakhurst and plan on a stopover at Lewis Creek Picnic Area. The "Moonlight Special" on Saturday summer nights adds barbecue and entertainment.

For more information:

Southern Yosemite Visitors Bureau, Box 1404, Oakhurst, CA 93644, 209-683-INFO.

Sierra Historic Sites Association, 209-683-6580.

Yosemite Mountain-Sugar Pine Railroad, 209-683-7273.

Eastern Madera Chamber of Commerce, 209-683-7766.

Golden Chain Theater, 209-683-7112.

53.

A Favorite Bass Lake

One of the best ways to get to Yosemite from Southern California is via Highway 41 from Fresno up through Oakhurst, but this route suffers one fatal defect—it by-passes Bass Lake. That's probably the reason why this popular lake isn't mobbed year-round instead of just in summer. So visit spring and fall when the weather and fishing peak and the campgrounds empty out. Note: If you must visit in summer, check out Eastman or Hensley lakes, which offer decent camping and uncrowded aquatic diversions.

There's a host of water sports here. You can bring or rent jet-skis, mini speedboats, party barges, water-ski boats, fishing craft, paddle boats, row-boats, or canoes. There are water-ski lessons and a batch of other options. This is the reason we rise at dawn to fish during the warmer part of the year, even though the lake is big enough for all sorts of activities.

We particularly enjoy a party barge jammed with kids of various vintages. A barge provides the best access to the best swimming spots in isolated coves, plus offers barbecues and, if you can't stand the wind in the pines, a stereo. These big platform boats are a nice choice for casual anglers. If you just want to look at the lake, try the *Bass Lake Queen II* which replaced the original wooden craft. She offers nifty cruises on the lake most summer afternoons around 4:00. She's a typical houseboat hull that seats fifty but floats a hundred; so head for the boardwalk on the north shore behind the Pines Restaurant a bit early. While Bass Lake's scenery may lack the grandeur of Yosemite an hour up the road, it suited filmmakers of *The Great Outdoors,* the John Candy and Dan Aykroyd comedy. A number of Westerns have been shot in the area, too.

Fishing in the fall for kokanee or for trout the rest of the year suits casual anglers, although this isn't really a prime fishing lake. It's better suited to kicking back on the shore or simply zipping over the water.

Since Bass Lake, at 3,300 feet is just about at the snowline in winter, the campgrounds are available all year at Wishon Point with reservations. Other campgrounds reserve in the summer, for a ten-day minimum stay. Our preference order for campgrounds is Spring Cove, Forks, Wishon, and Lupine-Cedar. Bass Lake's also a wonderful spot for big gatherings. The last two campgrounds mentioned offer two family sites, and there are group camps available for reservation May through mid-September (open for reservations early in January).

Bass Lake offers more than aquatic pleasures. There are hiking trails along Willow Creek that run past Angle Falls and Devil's Slide waterfalls and a nice trout stream. It's rather slick here, so watch the rocks near the creek! You also can survey the area from Goat Mountain Lookout off Spring Cover and from the Goat Mountain Trails that start in the Forks Campground on the south shore of the lake. There's even a nice spring about two miles in for a cool drink halfway to the lookout's splendid views. A shorter option that suits kids is the campground-to-campground hiking trail that's more level and only a couple of miles long.

The rest of your stay depends on the season. You'll find gold-panning championships, loggers' jamborees, arts and crafts festivals, ethnic outings, and more. (Check for current dates with the

Chamber of Commerce.) We're particularly fond of the Gathering of Warbirds at the Madera Airport toward the end of summer; this offers all sorts of old planes, parachuting, and military displays.

Whenever you visit, a convenient location's a big attraction at Bass Lake. If you camp or stay in a lake resort, or at Oakhurst or Madera, you're an easy drive from Yosemite, Big Trees, and at least six other lakes in the area. There's skiing within an hour or so and the "Ridge of Light" off to the east—the elevation is just high enough to be cool in the summer and low enough to avoid most winter snows. It's a lake for all seasons.

For more information:

Bass Lake Chamber of Commerce, Box 126, Bass Lake, CA 93604, 209-642-3676.

The Central Sierras

54.

Yosemite Off-Season

Only during off-season can you find the Yosemite John Muir so loved. Autumn gilds meadow and woodland foregrounds against granite cliffs, and animals put on their heaviest coats of the year. Winter dusts Half Dome with snow and, while skiers flood cross-country trails and Badger Pass downhill runs on the valley rim, the floor remains serenely uncrowded. Early-spring visits find waterfalls at maximum flow and meadows greening up for the crowds to come. Stroll to Yosemite Falls sans crowds, watch deer and wildlife prepare for cold weather, or just savor the valley. Add to that the savings on lodgings after November 1 and an easy drive to the park over highways that rarely require chains, and you simply lack an excuse to visit America's favorite alpine valley.

Like many, I switched to the Yosemite high country to avoid the crowds of the '60s and '70s. When I discovered that trout fishing at Yosemite peaks in the fall and the cross-country ski-track system offers lovely winter diversions, my wife, Annette, and I returned to my favorite valley to survey changes for ski articles.

We discovered a Yosemite dressed in clean skirts to welcome visitors, a Yosemite with a one-way road network to eliminate summer gridlock and improve off-season vistas, both at the price of a little map reading that avoids spousal comments such as "Dear, that's the second time we've passed Yosemite Falls."

We found campgrounds with clean, well-spaced sites and well-cared-for public facilities. Both seem major improvements over the old jam-them-in sites at the price of reservations during peak periods.

We enjoyed a wide range of accommodations and food. What we couldn't find was a beer can, soda bottle, or trashed garbage can in the whole valley. A deposit requirement solved the litter problem; relocating garbage-eating bears improved sanitation and visitor safety.

While it's easy to drive on uncrowded valley roads during winter's off-season, on our last visit we parked at the classic Ahwahnee Hotel built in 1927. It may rank as the best-run hotel in any national park. Shuttle buses took us to downhill and cross-country skiing and ice skating, and it's a quick and easy drive to other pleasures such as the Mariposa Grove's giant sequoias just an hour from the valley and offering snow-dusted solitude in the winter.

During our traditional anniversary room-service dinner, a very special meal indeed at the Ahwahnee, our waiter noted, "Flatlanders own Yosemite during the summer; locals take it back in the autumn and don't give it up until spring ends." This definitely seems to be the case, but we plan to steal a bit of Yosemite for ourselves at least once a winter.

Accommodations run more than $100 a night, but you enjoy the finest accommodations in the valley. Even if you don't lodge there, you should consider a meal in the massive main dining room. We've enjoyed afternoon high teas, lovely public rooms, and impeccable service here. Special activities include wine-tasting weekends and the exceptional Christmas dinner. Reservations always required! (The Christmas dinners fill more than one year ahead!)

The Yosemite Lodge offers typical motel-type accommodations, a central location, and lovely views of Yosemite Falls and El Capitan. Other lodgings offer a wide range of accommodations. RV campgrounds with hookups can be found just outside Yosemite at Wawona, El Portal, or Yosemite West.

Valley meals generally reflect the high quality of the associated lodgings. The Ahwahnee's dressy main dining room requires a coat, and food and prices rank with San Francisco's best. Save with less-expensive breakfast visits and enjoy the splendid view of El Capitan from the dining room. In milder weather, visitors enjoy drinks or snacks on the deck behind the hotel. Curry Village has fast food and cafeteria food; Yosemite Lodge feeds guests at two restaurants, a cafeteria, and an ice-cream parlor.

Like lively nightlife? You're on your own. We always spend so much energy skiing, fishing, or hiking during the day that we're too beat for much more than the scenic films at the hotel. We know naturalists give talks and there are meet-your-instructor ski nights, but not for us.

Like most return visitors, we observe a traditional pattern after we unpack in fall or spring. We work out travel kinks with a short hike up to Mirror Lake around Washington Column or to Happy Isles, where we catch a shuttle bus back to Curry Village or our lodgings. The shuttle passes the stables, where rides on well-behaved horses and burrows suit spring-to-fall visitors. If you wish to enjoy the splendid Yosemite back country come summer, you need to book a ranger-led High Sierra Camp or private pack trip now. In fact, even backpackers need summer reservations to avoid congestion.

If you plan a fall horseback or backpack trip, you can avoid crowds and enjoy prime Indian-summer weather after Labor Day. We used to backpack often, but always carried a radio for weather reports, as you must sometimes rush to the road when a storm heads in. Do check the weather before and during your trip so you can avoid the need for chains.

First-time visitors should drop in at the visitor center and pick up a copy of the informative "Yosemite Guide," which details seasonal offerings. The valley shuttle tour takes a couple of hours and seems the best way to discover the valley. Keeping your eyes on the road as you drive definitely tests your concentration! An audiovisual presentation, dioramas, and other exhibits explain the unique glacier-scoured geology of the valley and show how its small area relates to the many-times-larger Sierra High Country beyond the rim.

Curry and Yosemite Villages offer all services, shopping, and more so you need not rough it in the valley even in winter. Because we find Yosemite food and other prices on the high side, we buy supplies in valley towns such as Merced or Fresno before we drive into Yosemite.

My favorite activity, trout fishing, starts near El Portal on the Merced River, well downstream from the more populated east end of the valley. I find trout anxious to hit a fly or lure in the fall and cooperative during winter and early spring in the special-regulations areas. Light gear and insulated waders suit cold water, but the big problem for me remains concentration. Even compulsive trout addicts find it tough to keep their heads down and eyes on the hatch when El Capitan looms over the water. Back-country fishing in High Sierra lakes seems the better summer choice.

Fall horseback rides

My wife would rather hike than fish. She claims, "We get fish at home, but you can't walk through scenery like this anywhere else in the world!" All sorts of short trails suit hikers. Start in midmorning when ice melts, wear warm, waterproof shoes, plan to return before 3:00 in the afternoon to avoid the evening chill, and you can enjoy all sorts of trips.

My wife's favorites include "baby hikes," such as the easy walk into the wildly varied ice cornices at the base of Yosemite Falls, several loops to Mirror

Lake, and a variety of trails through valley meadows and woods along the Merced River. Guided hikes with a naturalist can add special flavor and a lot of information to your hiking day.

You can hike most days even in winter because it snows enough to stick on the valley floor only three or four times during the season. So don't expect snow in the valley. Only lucky visitors enjoy the chance to photograph snow-covered valley vistas or ski or snowshoe along meadow hiking trails. You can, however, enjoy scenic ice skating (rentals available) on an outdoor rink morning, afternoon, or night under Glacier Point. If the moon's up, do consider moonlight skates or strolls. Don't forget gloves and a warm jacket!

Most winter visitors to Yosemite spend their days at the snow sports center at Badger Pass, the oldest ski area in California and one that suits beginners and intermediates. It offers more of a settled, European ambiance than most ski areas and is just twenty-three miles from the valley via a shuttle bus. Family skiing doesn't get much better, and kids can't stray as far as they can at larger areas. Area ski instructors seem especially patient with older skiers new to the sport. Packages that include lessons and lift tickets can cut your costs here. Special kids' packages let the small fry learn fast and also free parents so they can enjoy their downhill day.

The Nordic Area offers ten miles of tracks leading to Glacier Point's incredible winter vistas. There are tracks to keep skis pointed in the right direction and reduce your effort per mile. More than ninety miles of trails wind through the rim and through the Mariposa Grove of Big Trees. First time skiers should start with a package that includes lessons and rentals to reduce effort and risk of injury.

Snow conditions permitting, more experienced cross-country skiers can enjoy snow camping, winter-survival seminars, overnight ski trips, and for the skilled and hardy, Trans-Sierra slogs. Visitors new to snow country might rent snowshoes for short, quiet jaunts beside cross-country trails. Trips longer than a couple of miles can leave you walking like a cowboy, but risk of injury seems minimal. Frankly, cross-country skiing is less work and safe if you start with lessons. Start with ranger-led snowshoe hikes or Yosemite mountaineering excursions. More sedentary visitors can ride rather noisy snow cats from Badger Pass Ski Area to the valley rim or watch the skiers from the lodge.

Snow, or rather its quarantine on the valley rim, makes Yosemite visits especially attractive. Drive in on Highway 41 from Fresno or on Highway 120, known as the Big Oak Flat Road, from Manteca, and you may face snow and, at times, chain requirements. Wind in on Highway140 through El Portal from Merced, and most years you won't even see much snow until you reach the Arch Rock entrance to the valley. The winding Tioga Pass Road to Lee Vining and Highway 395 closes in the winter. It accesses the famous High Camp Loop or day-hike camps at Tuolumne Meadows.

Admittedly, Yosemite isn't uncrowded all winter. Lodges fill during holidays and some weekends after Badger Pass opens. But skiers usually don't stay in the valley. So you can drive in and park to take public shuttles or drive even the largest motor coach into the valley and, with an eye on the weather, enjoy Yosemite at your own speed.

For more information:

National Park Service, Yosemite National Park, CA 95389.

Park Hotline camps, 209-372-4454. Yosemite Valley Visitor Center, 209-372-4845. Bus Tours, 209-372-1240 (Valley Floor, Moonlight, Mariposa Grove, etc., subject to snow and road conditions; call on arrival).

Yosemite Park and Curry Company, Yosemite National Park, CA 95389.

Hotel and other reservations, 209-252-4848.

Yosemite Natural History Association, Box 545, Yosemite National Park, CA 95389, 209-372-4532 (art activity center: photo and art workshops through December).

Yosemite Area Tourism Council, Fish Camp, CA 93623, 209-683-7273. Ask for booklet "Around Yosemite's Front Door."

Ticketron (camping reservations up to eight weeks in advance).

55.

Ski Yosemite

My father drove an RV into Yosemite in 1897. They called them sheepherder's wagons then and visitors stayed in the valley for weeks. Today, visitors mob up from spring to fall. Only in the winter can you enjoy Yosemite the right way—sans crowds. Rumor has it that RVs stay away in the winter because drivers don't like snow. The fact is simple—you rarely get great amounts of snow in the valley or on entry roads. However, you can drive up to Badger Pass and enjoy all the usual snow sports.

Winter snow bleaches the battleship-gray granite walls of Yosemite and builds massive ice cones below waterfalls. The valley rests from summer crowds. Aspens lace the view now bare of autumn's gold leaves. Cross-country skiers and snowshoers come for the miles of trails and tracks along the rim of the valley. Alpine skiers enjoy short family runs at Badger Pass, the oldest ski area in California. The fit and frisky enjoy snow camping, winter-survival seminars, and overnight ski trips.

More sedentary visitors enjoy one-hour snow-cat tours, photographing winter vistas, or taking "chefs' holidays." Ice skaters whirl and twirl below Half Dome. As night falls, some reluctantly drive out of the valley to RV campgrounds over toward Merced. Others stay overnight at the classic Ahwahnee, deluxe Yosemite Lodge, or economy Curry Village. There's no better place and no better time to enjoy the Sierras with, but not in, snow.

Ahwahnee Excellence: We treasure our stays at the Ahwahnee. Nothing beats a candlelit room-service dinner served in five slow courses in front of a romantic fireplace in your suite, unless, of course, it's the views of Yosemite in winter. Last visit, we started with smoked salmon, moved to Madeira consomme, then enjoyed asparagus salad, fillets Rossini with trimmings, and finished with chocolate mousse with Grand Marnier.

Complimentary afternoon teas with live music from 5:00 to 5:30 P.M. and after-dinner demitasses from 7:30 to 10:00 add an air of elegance to your stay. Movies and some of the finest hotel food anywhere in California show that the loving care that was expended in the building of this splendid hotel back in 1927 continues in its food-service area. If possible, try for fall wine tastings, winter weekends with visiting chefs, and other delicious attractions.

Any valley visitor should take at least one meal in the rustic formal Ahwahnee dining room. Breakfast is both hearty and considerably less expensive than dinner, but any meal or stay at the

Ahwahnee produces special memories to compound the remarkable vision etched by a Yosemite winter visit.

No other winter Sierra destination offers such easy road access without chains and the chance to see and enjoy snow without shoveling, since it rarely snows more than a foot or two in the Valley. However, do carry chains, just in case. (See Chapter 54, Yosemite Off-Season.)

Wise visitors keep an ear out on the weather and head home early when very large storms are forecast. Otherwise, winter visitors simply park at their lodgings and use park shuttles to reach ski areas and other attractions.

No Snow Choices: If you find the usual bare ground in the valley, brisk hikes set you up for meals. On windless days, hearty souls bike valley roads. Rental bikes are usually available from Yosemite Lodge, weather permitting. The path from Curry Village to Yosemite Lodge offers safe biking away from cars. We find the four and four-tenths mile Happy Isles/Mirror Lake Trail even more scenic.

Bus tours (again, weather permitting) circle the valley in daylight, but those who bundle up for the moonlight tour won't regret the trip. Half-day trips to the Mariposa Grove of Giant Sequoias let you see these massive giants without crowds and, if you are lucky, with a dusting of snow. Take lots of photos. You can get print film and Ektachrome (E6 process) developed and printed in a couple of hours with pickups at any lodgings.

Outstanding trout fishing in the Merced River is from late October through the spring runoff, usually in late March. Bring small dark flies and check on special regulations in force inside the valley and around El Portal all year.

Other seasonal activities make the valley even more attractive to visitors. Clinics and NASTAR races, Santa skis, movies, crafts programs, caroling, Easter-egg hunts, and more bring you up to the April winter carnival, an end-of-the-season fling with costume contests, races, a barbecue, and torchlight parade. Older skiers enjoy the Ancient Jocks Race, a fun event for those over thirty with a beer stop halfway down the course at Badger Pass. Visitors not exhausted by daylight activities can enjoy the traditional Thursday night ski buffet and dance at the Yosemite Lodge from January through March.

Cooks may want to try the January Chefs' Holidays. Weekend gourmet cooking classes packaged with stays at either the Ahwahnee or Yosemite Lodge feature guest chefs and regional specialties. (Call the Holiday Hotline, 209-454-2020, for information.)

Other Lodging Options: The Yosemite Lodge prices run lower than the Ahwahnee, with typical hotel accommodations and quite satisfactory meals. The location is just a long look from Yosemite Falls.

Curry Village suits even tighter budgets with rooms, cabins, and tent cabins along the Merced River. Tent cabins sleep up to six with a double bed, table and chairs, food-preparation area, a wood-burning stove, and nearby restrooms.

For more information:

National Park Service, Yosemite National Park, CA 95389.

Road information recording, 209-372-4605.

Park Hotline camps, etc., 209-372-4454.

Yosemite Valley Visitor Center, 209-372-4845.

Bus Tours, 209-372-1240 on arrival (Valley Floor, Moonlight, Mariposa Grove, etc., subject to snow and road conditions).

Yosemite Park and Curry Company, Yosemite National Park, CA 95389, 209-252-4848, for hotel and other reservations.
Art Activity Center, Yosemite Natural History Association, Box 545, Yosemite National Park, CA 95389, 209-372-4532 (photo and art workshops, spring through fall).
Yosemite Area Tourism Council, Fish Camp, CA 93623, 209-683-7273; ask for booklet *Around Yosemite's Front Door*.
Yosemite Mountaineering School, Yosemite National Park, CA 95389 (rock- and snow-climbing classes).
The Ansel Adams Gallery, Box 455, Yosemite National Park, CA 95389, 209-372-4413, for Photo Workshops.

Reading List: A good read can enrich your visit. John Muir's *Yosemite*, a 1912 guidebook, lets you see the valley as it was. *Cross Country Skiing in Yosemite* by Tim Messick covers nordic trails.

Ansel Adams's *Yosemite and the Range of Light* offers super black-and- white photographs. *Above Yosemite* by Robert Cameron lets you see the valley in wonderful color.

56.

Sequoia and Kings Canyon

Follow this if you can. Grant Grove, just inside the Big Stump entrance to General Grant National Park, doesn't have trees—just stumps, as it was logged back in 1890. (We'll skip General Grant National Park becoming part of Kings Canyon National Park, as that's too confusing.) Then consider the fact that nearby General Grant Tree is the world's third largest sequoia. But the second largest tree in the grove is named for General Lee. That makes sense, yes? However, why is the largest tree of all, over in Sequoia National Park, named after General Sherman?

In any case, the General's Highway, forty-five miles or so of winding road, gets you from one place to the other so you can puzzle this out on site. You can also enjoy rather a lot of trees that run to two hundred feet or so in height, and to twenty-five feet in diameter, and you'll hear, ad nauseam, that these aren't the same kinds of redwoods we'll meet over on the Coast. Poor trees! They used to be thought the oldest, but bristlecone pines took that.

What they are is unforgettable, if you take the proper steps to see them in the right time and place. That's not during summer in the heat of the day. Instead, try to visit the parks at dawn when the trees wear unearthly skirts of mist. Or ski in during winter months—several groves offer ski or snowshoe access even in big snow years. What you want to do is reduce the experience to that of Aristotle's ideal school: you on one end of the proverbial log and the tree on the other. At most, bring a friend who offers a scale, so you can see how big the trees are.

Picking the trees to see is easy. The Trail for All People runs a half mile in to the General Grant Tree, which offers an isolated statement of scale. To get a better sense of sequoias en masse, go four or five miles farther to Redwood Mountain Grove.

However, trees are just the start of the action. Kings Canyon, especially the deep canyons of the Kings River, offers some splendid outlooks and the chance to drive down Cedar Grove or Giant Grove Village. We used to spend a little time at the latter, as it was a fine takeoff to the back country, which has some of the best in California.

Sequoia National Park has its own attractions besides Giant Forest and its General Sherman Tree. Its lodgepole pines, with their huge cones, offer a classic pointy-tree look. It's too bad that logged-off lodgepoles are being replaced by other species in successive monoculture forests.

The key to enjoying both parks is, as always, during off-season visits. Spring, which can run into July in the higher elevations, greens the hills nicely. It starts when the snow melts and ice plants die. In most years, spring starts in May or June.

Fall, particularly in years with early rains, brings its own pleasures. Winter locks you out of some sections, depending on the weather. Summer can fry you down at Cedar Grove, so you need to plan to hike or fish early and late.

Fishing can be excellent in the Kings River, local streams, and a wide assortment of walk-in lakes up toward the Muir Trail. In season, and like the fishing this depends on snowfall and runoff, there's exceptional whitewater rafting (see Why Not White Water, Chapter 51).

Lodgings and other amenities in Kings Canyon and Sequoia National Parks vary from a dandy collection of campsites to the rather posh attractions of the Montecito-Sequoia Lodge. The less said about food at local snack bars or cafeterias the better, although copious seems a fair statement. Cottages at Cedar Grove Lodge offer summer lodging basics (some have bunk beds). Giant Forest Lodge offers basic motel accommodations and some tent cabins.

For more information:

Montecito-Sequoia Reservations Office, 800-227-9900.

For weather information, 209-565-3388.

57.

East Slope Excitement

Think of the Sierra Nevada, John Muir's Ridge of Light, as a wedge with its gradual Central Valley side sloping up to the peaks along the John Muir Trail before it drops off into the arid flats of the Great Basin or Owens Valley. I suppose I'm prejudiced. I grew up hiking summers in what's now the Emigrant Basin and in the mountains behind Bridgeport, where you'll find three easy entrances to the Hoover Wilderness off Highway 395.

Each entrance area is a weekend destination on its own. Virginia Lake, twelve miles south of Bridgeport, offers two dandy lakes with a lodge and campground, as well as a short hike to Frog and Crowley Lakes. If you're frisky, you can loop up into the peaks over a low pass and head back down to Green Creek's roadhead about seventeen miles away. You need a shuttle pickup to do this, but it's a nice two-day hike if you stop to fish at lakes that offer brook, brown, and rainbow trout.

From Twin Lakes, the travel presents a steep hike up to Crown Lake, Summit Lake Barney, and others, as well as the chance to hike over the divide to the Emigrant Wilderness Area and out to Pinecrest by way of Maxwell Lake, Emigrant Lake, and the other lakes in the area. This last hike seems like a four-day trip.

A fine pocket wilderness area offers a chance to sample the wilderness away from the dubious crowds that now shuffle up the John Muir and Pacific Crest Trails. All off these spots offer high-peak vistas. The U. S. Forest Service topographic map for the area's aptly named Matterhorn Peak, because from the north it looks like its Swiss namesake.

There are a couple of other interesting access points into the High Sierra. We like to drive off the Sonora Pass Road toward Leavitt Lake and, after a campsite rest to acclimate ourselves, hike up and over the long ridge between the West Walker River and Kennedy Lake to High Emigrant. From here, you can either hike for two days to Kennedy Meadows via Upper, Middle, and Emigrant Lakes or head back toward Bond Pass and the East Slope.

All of these areas have wonderful trout fishing, decent wilderness campsites (always purify your water), and fairly easy hiking. Supplies are available in Bridgeport, where there's a decent Basque restaurant, as well as motels and other offerings.

There are, of course, other East Slope options. However, most of these are rather crowded. Reds Meadows east of Yosemite, the Desolation Wilderness on the west bank of Lake Tahoe, and the very popular Tuolumne Meadows at the top of the seasonal Tioga Pass Road are secondary choices. Unfortunately, you need wilderness permits these days.

For more information:
Toiyabe National Forest, Bridgeport District, Bridgeport, CA 93517, 714-932-7070.

58.

Hanging Yourself—Rock Climbing, Mountaineering, and More

Rock climbing, "because it's there" or for other reasons, suits today's active weekender. It's a relatively inexpensive sport, requires decent physical conditioning, and, with the new indoor climbing walls, something you can do for years. It's also very, very safe if you learn the basics correctly and know your limits.

Once again, I'm prejudiced. I started climbing as a teenager and quit after age fifty when various body parts retired early. In the years between, I managed to get up quite a few peaks and rather a lot of Yosemite's climbs. Yosemite is, because of its wonderful granite, perhaps the birthplace of high-tech, high-technique American climbing. My father's friend John, whose first ascent of the valley's Lost Arrow, a spire still a worthwhile challenge, helped develop some of the early climbing aids.

Today, climbing seems vastly improved and much, much more organized. So it's easy to learn. Do realize that balance and "true grit" seem more important than strength or macho. Some of the best climbers are women. If you can get women instructors, they always seem more skilled and more patient than the men.

One of the best climbing schools in the world is the Yosemite Climbing School, perhaps the only reason I know for visiting the valley in summer. Another climbing school worth a mention is at the top of Donner Pass—check it out in the old Donner-Spitz lodge on "old 40" out of Norden off Interstate 80.

Yosemite, like most schools, runs basic rock-climbing classes, then moves to intermediate and more advanced classes as required. It also offers advanced climbing, alpine survival, avalanche recognition, and snow and ice climbing, as well as oddments such as Trans-Sierra ski treks and more. For now, consider a climbing weekend.

I'd start in Yosemite on the best rock in the world. Wander under El Cap where the climbers' campground demonstrates not everyone of college age joined the MBA quest. You can watch some basic boulder climbing and get an idea of how far the fit and frisky can wriggle their way up the rocks and sheer stone walls.

Then head over to Curry Village to sign up for the class in fall, spring, or winter and check on renting climbing shoes. During summer, the classes start up in Tuolumne Meadows. Note: Most Yosemite hotels have information. About the only requirement is "reasonable physical condition" and "at least fourteen years old." Note for parents: Climbing classes can be the solution to bored teenagers who claim there's "nothing to do" in the valley.

Classes start around 8:30 A.M. with basics, such as moving only one hand or foot at a time, and instructors work on making you feel more comfortable about leaning back from the rocks sometimes to be safest. Individual attention and plenty of time to rest should leave you feeling fit and frisky as classes end in the afternoon.

You'll find similar weekend classes out of the Mountain Shop in Truckee, in South Tahoe, and out of Sonora. All climbing schools require permits from the Forest or Park Services, you can be sure that instructors are qualified and operations are insured. This is something that looks a lot more dangerous than it is. Best of all, a day on the slabs makes wonderful war stories when you go back to work or school on Monday.

59.

Boarded with Skiing

If you want to try something besides downhill skiing on your snow trips, and find cross-country skiing too tame, try a snowboard. This is easier than it looks, as the board keeps your feet in the right place and you don't mess with ski poles. The "Airport" snowboard park on the Nevada side of

South Lake Tahoe has all sorts of nifty runs, tubes, and pipes, and you'll find "Shred Ready" schools both at the nearby Boulder and California Lodges. There's even a "Boardinghouse" next to Long's Drugs on Highway 50.

No-Snow Shows: South Lake Tahoe offers winter attractions even for those who don't ski. Winter brings big-name entertainers like Frank Sinatra to South Tahoe show rooms. Stage shows such as *42nd Street* hit the boards here, too. We do find the later cocktail shows a bit more lively than dinner offerings, but some of the best acts are in lounges and piano bars, where new talent discoveries make their mark. Discos, western bars, and dance halls finish off the night-life set.

Days can fill with shopping, dog-sled or sleigh rides, cruises on the lake, and visits to Carson City, Nevada's capital, with fine museums and much else. Granted you pay the price of a bit of strip-mall zoning on the California side, but you can find plenty to do even if you don't ski. And, of course, there are always the slots and tables!

Getting There: The easy way in from Northern California is on Highway 50 if you consider chains and such. When the weather's more questionable, many drive in over Interstate 80 and come down through Nevada or along the eastern side of Lake Tahoe.

If you fly in, Reno's Cannon International Airport runs shuttle buses and rents winterized cars, either 4WDs or front-wheel models with chains. Unless there are four or more in your group, consider the shuttle. It's about an hour and a quarter to South Lake Tahoe. You also can take TW Express flights from Los Angeles or San Francisco to South Tahoe Airport, about ten minutes from town.

Getting Around: Between the Heavenly Valley ski area's free ski shuttle from most South Tahoe lodgings, the free casino shuttles, and Tahoe Area Regional Transit buses, there's little need for a car unless you plan to ski other areas with Heavenly "interchangeable" lift tickets. Don't overlook sternwheeler or sailboat tours in fall or spring, either.

Food and Lodgings: Casinos offer more food and lodging for less even if you don't gamble. You'll find 11,500 housing units, and all of them will be absolutely packed during holidays. So book early. We've had good luck with Heavenly Valley's central reservations. Do ask about their winter lift/lodging packages and, in particular, the special discounts that run early and late in the season.

60.

Ski Heavenly

Lift tickets cost more each year, so it's a good thing Heavenly Valley lets you save on gambler-subsidized food and lodgings just minutes away in South Tahoe.

Has it been more than forty years since Heavenly Valley opened its slopes in 1955 at what many considered the wrong end of Lake Tahoe? Must have been, as that was the theme for last year. Not that Heavenly needs a special theme. With the azure waters of Lake Tahoe on one side and the colorful high deserts of Nevada and the green ranch lands of the Carson Valley on the other, Heavenly would be worth a visit even if it didn't have the longest run and highest vertical in the Tahoe basin. It's also a superb place to introduce new skiers to the snow for, if the trail doesn't take, the area has more than enough "no- ski" activities to keep anyone interested. But for skiers, the only problem once you reach the top of the tram is trail selection.

There's a choice of wide-groomed slopes, twisty expert runs, and neat open bowls with varied east, north, west, and south exposures. You always can find decent snow somewhere. Best of all, at least for those who don't gamble, you can find luxury, but affordable, lodgings in any of a number of Nevada-side casinos. Gamblers pay the freight. And you enjoy the inexpensive buffets, solid restaurants, and rather nifty shows as well.

These, plus the free shuttles to the slopes can radically cut your package costs for a weekend or weeklong stay. So can avoiding car-rental costs. Stick with the free shuttles and cabs unless you want to sample Thai's North Shore ski areas such as Squaw Valley, Alpine Meadows, or Sugar Bowl up at the top of Donner Pass. Of course, casinos bet you can't resist the temptations of the tables. How certain are they? Most offer free twenty-four-hour shuttles to and from the slopes daily.

One thing seems certain: With so much night life, skiers who hit the twenty-five Heavenly Valley lifts when they open at 9:00 A.M.—8:30 on weekends and holidays—find plenty of untracked runs. There were seventy-nine in 1995, with a mix of twenty percent beginner, forty-five percent intermediate and thirty-five percent advanced and expert. And there's plenty of space with nearly five thousand patrolled acres that enjoy a "paltry" three hundred inches average snowfall that's supplemented by a hundred and twenty inches' of machine-made snow that's shot onto two-thirds of the hill as needed.

Favorite runs are personal, but it's wise to loosen up with easy runs and work up to your ability level. End your day with easy runs, too—most injuries are early and late. Then, once you find that near-perfect run, ask the lift attendants to suggest more of the same. Hopefully, you'll ski Heavenly for enough days to learn how you can follow the sun around the mountain to stay with perfect snow conditions.

Like most top resorts, ski schools at Heavenly are popular enough to ensure that you ski with others of your ability. There are also special ski seminars and classes for women, seniors, and kids. The last have a "Magic Carpet" lift at the Children's Ski School.

Tip: Check out the Nevada side's nine lifts which often collect fewer bodies than the more scenic runs on the California side. If you ski with kids, either stick them in the kiddy ski school or limit them to runs on one side of the mountain, or you won't see them until dark!

For more information:

Heavenly Ski Resort, Box 2180, Dept. LBFT, Stateline, NV 89449, 800-2-HEAVEN. The ski-condition number is 916-541-SKI4 (7544) or 702-586-7000.

NORTHERN CALIFORNIA

Bay Area and Marin

61.

San Francisco, East of Van Ness

Today, it's difficult to realize that all of San Francisco east of Montgomery Street rests on fill—rocks and dirt from the hills that now cover the fleet of abandoned ships that carried the forty-niners west. California looks ahead, not back, and those new to the state often seem dreadfully ignorant of its history. No place is this more true than in San Francisco.

One route to a better appreciation of "Baghdad by the Bay" is William Camp's classic *San Francisco Port of Gold.* Another route to understanding is at the California Historical Society. Even the exceptional San Francisco Library offers keys to unlock the past and the realization that the comfortable stayed home. Those anxious to improve their lot came to the city by the Golden Gate.

Certainly, San Francisco has warts. Traffic downtown moves the same speed as it did when horses drew freight wagons—they double-parked in those days, too—and flatlanders find the hills challenging. It's expensive. It's crowded. Some neighborhoods aren't safe after dark. But it's also exciting, incredibly scenic, ethnic, and totally endearing. It's no accident that it ranks at the top of America's favorite cities.

If you're a first-time visitor, take a Gray Line or other half-day tour or drive the 49 Mile Drive.

A quick look at Golden Gate Park, the Palace of the Legion of Honor, Chinatown, North Beach, the Haight-Ashbury area, and Fisherman's Wharf lets you see what's where. Mark your map for later returns on foot. Then invest a day east of Van Ness. You may need two if you walk slowly!

Start with Union Square and try Gumps for Oriental gear, Nieman-Marcus for excess, Dunhill's for men's doodads, Saks or Magnin's for women's gear, and enough other fine shops to eat up an entire day for the shopping-impaired.

However, to understand and enjoy San Francisco best, "think ethnic" and get out of downtown, for it's not a melting pot; it's more of a stew. Grant Street centers Chinatown even though the laterals and parallels that have fewer tourist shops offer better prices. Stop for dim sum—the point-and-taste meals where you pay by the plate—on side streets such as Alder Place, where you'll find the Chinese Historical Society of America and upstairs restaurants where the Chinese eat. Then continue westward.

Cross Broadway and, with the obligatory look at Big Al's and memories of Carol Doda's silicon splendors, you'll find yourself in North Beach's Little Italy. Bocce, wonderful cafes where you can read the Sunday paper while the waiters sing arias, and a host of affordable family restaurants make the walker's day. If it's Sunday, it's time to relax. Try an espresso from a time before they were overshadowed by Starbucks or line up outside a Washington Square bakery to buy baguettes or "dark bake" bread to go with your cold cuts from Molanari's deli on Columbus.

If you're frisky, pick up the makings of a fine picnic at one of twenty Italian delis and head up the hill to Coit Tower, which one wag suggests,

San Francisco flower stand

"contains all the lousy spaghetti sauce in town that's piped downhill to cheap restaurants." History buffs will want to check on Mrs. Coit, who fought fires and smoked cigars. The murals and the elevator ride are recommended. The view's fine and free!

Intellectuals might want to browse City Lights Bookstore, which has spanned an era from the Beat Generation through the hippies to today, or down an espresso in the Trieste Cafe. Feet tired? Time's up? Head west and catch the cable car.

Otherwise, keep walking. Follow the cable-car tracks or the Muni bus line down to Fisherman's Wharf, the Cannery, Cost Plus, Pier 39, and more chances to shop until you drop. Don't worry about what's where; wander and explore. Eat on the fly. A crab Louie's traditional, and best in the winter months; abalone's a must at least one time—don't ask the price—and seafood's the choice. Walk out on Muni Pier to take a look at Alcatraz—a nice spot to visit if you have more time—otherwise, check the Hyde Street Pier's historic vessels that run from lumber schooners to side-wheel ferry boats.

Tired yet? If it's still light, catch the last boat tour on the Red & White or Blue & Gold fleet for a quick run on the bay, as the sun sets behind the Golden Gate.

After a day like this, you may want to sit out the evening, even though San Francisco's opera, ballet, theater, jazz, flamenco, or rock clubs and much, much more beckon. A bus back up Van Ness takes you to the delights of City Hall, the Opera House, and our favorite boutique hotel, the Inn at the Opera. However, you may want to leave this area for another day and substitute it with a few hours at a street-front cafe table on Broadway or Vallejo or Columbus Avenue. These offer world-class people-watching, too.

62.

San Francisco, West of Van Ness

There's another San Francisco that tourists only sample on the ocean side of Van Ness. This is the wide avenue left by the firebreak that eventually stopped the fires which caused most of the damage in the 1906 earthquake. As a result, many intersections in town now are built over huge water-filled cisterns so that, when the next great quake breaks water mains, there will be water to spare for the fires.

The San Francisco of neighborhoods does offer its own tourist attractions.

There's no better half day for kids than the Exploratorium, which lurks behind the city's swan-filled pools as the only remaining artifact of the San Francisco Exposition. The marina's also a splendid spot to fly kites, see boats moored in the Saint Francis Yacht Club, or watch racing sailboats. The local Safeway is like none other as a spot to pick up picnic makings or, according to a single's source, "dates of all genders."

Farther along, through the now demilitarized Presidio, you'll come to Fort Point and its namesake fortification. Then you cut back toward the Golden Gate Park and the joys of Clement Street. Clement follows Anza and Balboa—streets are alphabetical one way, and avenues climb up to 48th.

Golden Gate Park deserves its own weekend and certainly most of a day. If you must spend less time, start with the M. H. De Young Memorial Museum. Sunday's nice, as JFK Drive and other streets close for hikers, bikers, and roller-bladers, and there's a Muni Band Concert as well. The Asian Art Museum next door, which some call "The Brundage Collection," is one of the best in the world, and you can rest your feet at a tea service at the Japanese Tea Garden.

With more time, or if you've a mechanical bent, walk across the Music Concourse and check out the California Academy of Sciences. It sports Steinhart Aquarium, the oldest aquarium in the United States, a decent planetarium, wild-animal halls, and a batch of other things of interest. All of these spots charge admission, but a "culture pass" gets you into everything once and, if you run out of time, it's good for a year.

There's a lot more in the park. The redwoods and Garden of Fragrance in the Stybring Arboretum and Botanical Gardens behind the band shell at the end of the Music Concourse offer a good free look at over six thousand different species of plants. Gardeners also appreciate the Conservatory of Flowers, sort of a scale model of England's Kew Gardens, and it's inexpensive and definitely worth the price.

Most people miss out on the San Francisco Casting Club pools with their free lessons and polo games on some Sundays. Add the Dutch windmills at the beach, meadows where the hippies once gathered, and along the long "panhandle" that attaches to the park, Haight-Ashbury and its now graying flower children left over from the 1969 Summer of Love.

At this point, you've long since run yourself out of daylight, and it's time to head back to your lodgings. As an alternative to downtown's famous hotels such as our favorite Ritz or St. Francis, consider an inexpensive motel toward the San Francisco Zoo at the beach or off Geary Boulevard, or even a stay in Japantown.

Japantown, between the Filmore and Pacific Heights, sports a cobbled Japan Center Mall along the three blocks of the Japan center that runs to sushi and a selection of Japanese goods. Check the small hardware store across the street which has got some dandy tools and gadgets. Bentos and various seafood and other items rolled in rice and seaweed suit the experiment-minded.

From here, it's an easy trip on Filmore Street up through the upscale mansions of Pacific Heights and down to Cow Hollow's Union Street, perhaps the most interesting shopping street in San Francisco. Union's a dandy spot to walk, with the best shops, galleries, and restaurants toward Gough, a block from Van Ness.

You're still far from running out of neighborhoods. Clement Street offers solid shopping and dining on its first twenty blocks. The Latin beat of the Mission deserves a look, and the Filmore's a dandy spot for ribs and such.

It's here in the neighborhoods that you find San Francisco. There are others, too. Polk Gulch, on both sides of the California Street cable-car line, and the Castro District deserve attention, too. A series of interesting neighborhoods run along Geary Boulevard all the way to the beach. Then there's a chance to hike the beach, brunch at the Cliff House, or visit the Zoo. So invest a weekend west of the tourists and you'll see that old-time San Francisco, like the pioneers, has simply migrated west.

Addendum—Eating in San Francisco: The latest spots vary, but over the years the following have been good. Scoma, for seafood, is near but not on Fisherman's Wharf; Jack's, on Sacramento Street, is noted for the double entrees; Tadishes Cold Day Grill, for the sturgeon; and the Washington Square Bar and Grill, for the calamari. All moderate.

You can spend more at Kans for upscale Chinese food; check out the newest food fads at Stars. Consider the special "two people, ten entrees and ten wine samples" at the Ritz, or hit traditional French food at five-star Ernie's.

However, the joy of San Francisco foods—the seafood, sourdough French bread, and interesting ethnic dishes—come just as readily from small spots in the neighborhoods, and guides to such restaurants seem a popular local industry.

63.

Time for Tomales

The only fault one can find with Tomales Bay is the San Andreas Fault that forms the bay as it runs along the ocean bottom. Few Northern Californians appreciate the fact that Point Reyes is geologically part of L.A. Eventually, one supposes, Point Reyes will move up the coast to Eureka or, perhaps, Seattle. In the meantime, Tomales Bay offers sailing, boating, clamming, and fishing inside the shelter of Point Reyes, now part of a wonderful National Seashore that runs down to San Francisco.

Point Reyes offers one lighthouse, two main access roads, at least three beaches, four kinds of clams, five parking lots, six Inverness Inns and b and bs, and a host of elk and other animals, plus birds. With so much to see, staying in Inverness or up the road at the posh Inn of the Tides in Bodega Bay makes sense. The latter includes breakfast at a wonderful indoor/outdoor pool and features romantic rooms that can include fireplaces. All this just across Highway 1 from the bay and a decent restaurant.

If you must visit for one day only, you can wind up and over Mount Tamalpais on Highway 1 past Stinson Beach—a stop at the Sand Dollar Cafe's good for coffee and pastry. You might check the great blue herons on Bolinas Lagoon and at the Audubon Ranch during spring mating season. Skip Bolinas, as there's little parking and less welcome for tourists these days; stay north on Highway 1. In a hurry to get home? Try Petaluma-Point Reyes Road back from Highway 1 to Highway 101.

To see what's where at Point Reyes, check Olema's Visitors Center to look at maps of the geology and history of the area. Olema is also a shortcut to Limantour Beach and its estuary, both offering peak bird-watching in the spring or fall during migrations. However, the best route through the park runs along Sir Francis Drake Highway through Inverness, where there's good food, nice lodgings, rental boats, and more.

The highway and its bay were named after Queen Elizabeth I's favorite "pirate." Drake careened his ships on the shore of Drake's Bay in order to remove barnacles, seaweed, and, worse, that otherwise slowed them down. Fortunately for Drake, the local Indians were friendly. One can only suppose his sailors stayed out of ocean waters off Point Reyes Beaches, for these bite the unwary with icy water, riptides, undertows, and, yes, one of the largest concentrations of great white sharks in the North Pacific.

After a stop at the visitor center, a walk on whichever beach is least windy, a check to see if the gray whales are in sight, and perhaps a visit to the lighthouse, head back into Tomales Bay to swim. You'll spot Tule elk, deer, and a host of other protected wildlife as you drive. So take it slow, get there early to ensure parking, enjoy your swim or hike, and then think about lunch or dinner.

In any season, a visit to Tomales is an excuse to pig out on seafood. You get your own if you bring a small boat and launch at the ramp near Marshall, where you can clam up your own horsenecks on the flats around Hog Island. You can scratch for cockle clams in the gravel a few steps from Highway 1; you can pull mussels from the rocks; and on the Point Reyes side of the bay, it's possible to pop oysters and, out on ocean rocks, go for the few abalone the sea otters have left. Bring shovels, rakes, tire irons, buckets, a fishing license, and a copy of the size and bag regulations. A spare set of dry clothing is handy, too. Or, you can take the clam barge over to the flats from Lawson's Landing.

Add some decent shore fishing for perch, smelt, striped bass, and salmon in the bay—a few steelhead even run here—then consider the excellent party-boat fishing for salmon and bottom fish from Bodega Bay just to the north.

Don't do it yourself? Johnson's Drake's Bay Oyster Farm sells oysters in cocktails and on the half shell. Better buys are their pints or quarts; remember that bigger isn't better with oysters! A number of exceptional restaurants in the area offer oysters in most modes. Two Czech restaurants, Vladimir's and Manka's, attract lots of hungry folks to Inverness, the quaint village halfway up the ocean side of the bay. Why two Czech restaurants? Ask!

Inverness is also a good spot for b and bs and inns, and there are rental sail- and other boats, as well as some exceptional craft shops and studios. It's a Carmel without tourists and particularly relaxing during the week, and if you're not shopped out, there's always Point Reyes Station, which is probably the westernmost Western town in the US. All you need are the cowboys and cattle drives!

The inland side of Tomales Bay offers more bucolic pleasures. Highway 1 hugs the shoreline on its way to Bodega Bay, but a number of lateral roads snake over green hills to Highway 101 and Petaluma. These roads offer better biking than Point Reyes, as the shoulders are wider and the hills are alive with the sound of sheep, California quail, and dairy cattle. This is a splendidly scenic area to search for the special foods that help make San Francisco chefs famous.

Free-range chicken, low-fat beef, farm quail, and, on the Point Reyes Road to Petaluma, the

"Rouge et Noir" delights of the Marin French Cheese Company punctuate your drive. Note: If you're driving up Highway 1 to Point Reyes from Petaluma, and that's the fast route from San Francisco and the Bay area, stop in Petaluma for some freshly baked French bread. There also are several exceptional delis and some wonderful fresh eggs. Add ducks, geese, homemade sausages, and a batch of seasonal fruits and vegetables, and you'll go home with gourmet delights for a week.

There's another route home, too. Just follow Sir Francis Drake Boulevard back up Papermill Creek toward Mill Valley and you'll discover what many locals consider "the other Muir Woods." Samuel B. Taylor State Park runs from redwoods into coastal transition zones of oaks and grass. There's even a swimming hole that's considerably warmer than the ocean and, if it's not too foggy, a number of decent hikes with ocean views.

For more information:
Inns of Point Reyes, 415-663-1420.
Inns of Marin, 415-663-9373.
Samuel B. Taylor State Park, 415-488-9897.
Tomales Bay State Park, 415-669-1140.

64.

Biking and Better in Sausalito

Most who vacation in the Bay Area stay in San Francisco. That's a decent approach, but a Sausalito stay puts a different spin on things. It best suits active visitors who walk, bike, or roller-blade in order to work off the calories doubtless ingested from fine local restaurants, bakeries, and food stands. Leave your vehicle where you stay to avoid the dubious joys of parking. Add splendid bay views, a chance to ferry over to San Francisco or Angel Island, and, if one insists, Muir Wood redwood trees or the sandy joys of Stinson Beach.

Each year, bikes, blades, and boots are bigger in California, and in no place in Northern California is this more true than in Marin County. This western county over toward Tomales Bay offers a network of what we used to call "sports-car" two-lane roads, but the best biking around has to be found on the trips from either San Francisco to Tiburon or the shorter run to or from Sausalito. You easily can take a ferry from Sausalito to San Francisco and bike back along the bay through the Marina District and up and over the Golden Gate Bridge. If the fog does not roll in, consider a picnic in the middle of the bridge. Then, after you crest the span, it's an easy coast back downhill into Sausalito. Note: During the week, wait until 10:00 A.M. for the later ferry to avoid rush hours.

There's an interesting side trip through the Waldo Grade Tunnel under Highway 101. There's a small lake north of the road toward the gravel beach. There's a road extension up and overlooking the Bay Bridge, and a dirt road to a tiny beach park and old-time gun emplacements. It's a short walk down to the water; it's much, much longer back up the hill, but a view of the Marina District under the Golden Gate repays the effort. Other attractions worth your time include the Marine Mammal Center, where they patch up sea otters, and the Point Bonita Lighthouse, which offers a killer view.

You can walk or roller-blade this route, too, but better hiking trails network Mount Tam and Muir Woods National Monument or run along the shores of Richardson Bay. Muir Woods is just off Highway 1 toward Stinson Beach, a nice spot for a drive and a worthwhile shore walk. Muir has at least fifteen hiking trails to suit all efforts. It's most attractive when the summer afternoon fog rolls in—*Star Wars* fans find *déjà vu* images—or at dawn or dusk before the crowds arrive.

Bikers should contemplate Mount Tam with respect. It's the spot where mountain biking really started when locals rode fat-tire bikes down fire trails until they discovered the brakes would not stand up to the steep grade. These days, Ridgecrest Boulevard takes as many bikers as sightseers to the top, where the best view of the Bay Area on the Marin side of Mount Diablo waits. Just pick a winter day after a storm that's neither smoggy nor foggy. Otherwise, watching the fog spill over the hills in early afternoon can highlight summer visits.

Tiburon—its ferry is an alternate route to San Francisco and enroute to Angel Island State Park—runs to yuppie boutiques and politically correct California cuisine. If you do not shop, you can always check the wildlife in the Richardson Bay Audubon Center. Expect lots of shore birds year-round and a wonderful collection of winter waterfowl. If you fish, stop at Elephant Rock or head along the frontage road north to small parks, upscale waterfront homes, and San Quentin State Prison. You can visit if you do not wear blue jeans—prisoners do that—and follow rather a lot of rules. Call ahead, as hours vary.

On the way back to Sausalito, stop at Frank Lloyd Wright's massive Marin County Civic Center (in San Rafael) off Sir Francis Drake Boulevard, and just off Highway 101. Call for tour reservations available during business hours to enjoy the fine points you might miss on self-guided tours.

With an extra day to invest, ferry over to Angel Island, which has been through more changes than a stripper, but it's a good summer-day picnic trip if whitecaps don't rough up the bay. It's worth the ferry fee, because the chug up to its highest point, Mount Livermore, offers 360-degree bay vistas. Good days are also a good time to try for striped bass, salmon, bottom fish, or sturgeon from party boats that head out from Sausalito and other Marin ports.

If the weather's lousy, and Sausalito collects summer fog, staying in town makes sense. Walk down Bridgeway behind the seawall and Benny Buffan's nifty statue of a seal. Check out the anglers and the views, and there's incredible people-watching around Ondine. It is also a dandy spot for deck meals on decent days. Note the change into upscale shopping that spills up the hill and into a series of malls and shops. Expect to spend a half day if you shop.

Then hike on past one of the better collections of "ragbag" and "stink boats" in America toward Richardson's Bay, the San Francisco Bay, and Delta Model. The latter offers a working hydraulic scale model with oddments such as a four-foot-long Golden Gate Bridge used to check on proposed bay and delta changes with its fifteen-minute tidal cycle, and flows that can be reversed to backtrack oil spills and such. The multimediia presentation is worth its ten minutes or so, and there are self-guided tours and enough else to eat up an hour or two. Tip: Bring fast film if you plan to take photographs.

Still frisky? Check out the wildly varied houseboats and ask about the amorous fish that croak loud enough to disturb the boaters.

Tired? Walk a block up the hill to a seat sans view in the locals' Sausalito, with its assortment of coffee shops, bakeries, and cafes that suit any taste and serve fine meals at much less than you'd pay in waterfront restaurants. Then it's back to the hill side of Bridgeway and a stop at the No Name Bar—no sign, but you can find it—where Sterling Hayden and Spike Africa plotted trips to the South Pacific. That's a story to investigate! After this, it's time to put the feet up.

Lodgings in Sausalito aren't cheap; San Rafael's a better budget option. Our favorite Casa Madrona is expensive but has wonderfully varied rooms with views right on up the hill from Bridgeway. The Alta Mira Hotel may be the best known in town, and it certainly has one of the most scenic decks and best restaurants. A host of b and bs that vary from year to year increases your choices.

Choices define Sausalito, from Sally Sanford, the one-time San Francisco madam who ran for mayor on the platform of "more Johns," to leftover beatniks and imitation mariners. It's a town of contrasts and choices that may offer California's best people-watching and a vacation of many memories.

For more information:
San Quentin Prison, 415-454-8808.
Marin County Civic Center, 415-499-6104.
Bay & Delta Model, 415-332-3871.
Casa Madrona, 415-332-0502.

65.

Close in at Carquinez

Far too many vacations trap you in a car for far too many hours. As a travel writer, my rather unflattering term for this is "tin-can travel." If you drive an hour or more to and from work each day, you don't need more car time. So here are Carquinez Straits diversions between Vallejo, and if you like, an extra day at Marine World, Africa USA, or

Martinez and the delta country. None of the above are more than an hour from most of the Bay Area, or each other, and barely more than that from Sacramento.

Carquinez Straits bears a vital, if usually ignored, place in California's history. It was the main water route to Sacramento and the Gold Country. More than two hundred sternwheelers chugged past en route to or from delta waters. The Pony Express ran mail by sternwheeler from Sacramento, and the main rail route once barged across the strait from Benicia to Port Costa. The former was even the capital of California for a time; the latter was once the largest grain shipping port in the world. Today, a scenic mix of container ships, fishing boats, pleasure craft, barges, and other nautical oddments crowd the waters.

Crockett and Port Costa on the south and Benicia to the north each offers a solid selection of activities and some interesting lodging and dining options. Add an hour or two visiting John Muir's house in Martinez and Vallejo's attractions, and you can fill a long weekend.

Crockett—Sugar and Fish: The massive waterfront C&H sugar refinery kept Crockett going after the Carquinez Bridge put the ferry boats out of business. Crockett's a classic California blue-collar town with a small collection of old-time-cafes that still serve decent coffee with refills and homemade pie, and some surpassingly nice antiques shops. It's a place of neatly cared-for homes and old-time values and a time machine to California as it was, and it's incredibly more relaxing than most tourist spots.

Not much happens, and that's as it should be. You can book a sugar refinery tour—this was a much bigger deal when C&H (California & Hawaii) refined Hawaiian sugar cane here than it is today when much of our sugar comes from beets. You can visit the small museum or head down to Dowrellio's wharf under the Carquinez Bridge and book a cooling summer-evening fishing trip for striped bass or sturgeon. Joey Pallota, who skippers a boat here, holds the world's record for sturgeon, and any sturgeon's a wonderful catch. Tip: The seafood's fresh, if simply prepared, at the wharf restaurant.

During the week, when the traffic's light, you can drive or bike east toward Port Costa and tourist country. The frontage road once ran all the way through to Benicia, although slides took it out regularly. Now it dead-ends just past Port Costa, so it's ideal for a kids' bike trip or a happy day with minimum traffic.

Port Costa—Grain and Railroads: Only a single massive concrete warehouse and some tide-washed pilings remain of the dozens of grain elevators and warehouses that once punctuated the brown hills along the strait. Port Costa's a time machine, a place only lately discovered by the Mercedes set who, with an odd mix of bikers and family visitors, wind down the hill and into the deep canyon that opens into Port Costa, the port that's no longer a port.

Today, it's a quiet town of contrasts. The Warehouse Bar and Restaurant serves lobster and beer to bikers and BMW types. The Bull Valley Inn runs to reservations-only crowds on weekends, and the collection of antiques, many connected with the town's railroad past, deserves a longer look. So do the many handcrafted redwood homes, the quiet streets, and, across the strait and the rail tracks that run at the water end of town, Benicia.

Benicia—Artists and History: Arts Benicia, a wonderful co-op of skilled artisans and artists, typifies today's Benicia better than its massive new marina and the homes, condos, and apartments on the hills where grain grew. The old industrial district around H Street offers glass blowers, neon artists, potters, and painters. This is fine arts, not T-shirt-store country, so come prepared to invest your time and money if you're serious about art. There's more art downtown on First Street.

For history buffs, the Benicia State Capitol and Historical Park at First and West G offers tours of the restored 1852 State House and the Fischer-Hanlon House. The Captain Walsh House Bed and Breakfast adds lodgings, and the Union Hotel's another worthwhile choice with a decent restaurant. Do park by the water and hike up the hill side of First Street, so it will be downhill back to the car. It'll take a half day to cruise the shops. Spouse doesn't shop? There's fishing off the pier at the end of the street or over at Dillon Point in Benicia State Park Recreation to the west, with wonderful picnic areas by the water. You can hike or bike along the Waterfront Parkway.

In the other direction, it's military history. There's even a Camel Barn Museum built by then Secretary of War Jefferson Davis to house the US Camel Corp. Add a clocktower fortress, commandant's home, and guardhouse, all conveniently near the artists' studios. All this comes with a view of Port Costa and the Carquinez and Martinez Bridges.

For more information:
Arts Benicia, 707-747-0131.
Benicia Chamber of Commerce, 707-745-2120.
Bull Valley Inn, 510-787-2244.
Camel Barn Museum, 707-745-5435.
Union Hotel, 707-746-0100.
Warehouse Restaurant, 510-787-1827.

66.

San Mateo and Peninsula Lighthouses

A solid peninsula weekend might lump Point Montera Lighthouse with Pigeon Point Lighthouse—both offer "light housekeeping" through the American Youth Hostel—with a visit to Santa Cruz Lighthouse, Santa Cruz, or the Santa Cruz Mountains. In the old days, keepers of the lights kept oil lamps burning, lenses polished, and the clockwork mechanisms turning. Now it's all done with electronics and sensors. However, lighthouses retain their romance year-round—during fall harvest season or in spring when lambs romp on the hills and flowers peak, during summer when the shore's a cool break, and even during winter when trips offer crashing surf. Caution: California's rocky shore sneaker waves drown a lot of innocents each year, so keep your distance. Some rocky shores are unstable or slippery or both.

Point Montera honked away with fog horns between 1875 and 1900, when the powers that be added an oil lantern. In 1912, a Fresnel lens offered more range—you can see a Fresnel lens in Monterey's Maritime Museum and read the explanation about how the grooved lens focuses the light.

While the 1872 Pigeon Point Light, named after the *Carrier Pigeon,* a ship wrecked at its foot, now has the usual bright strobelike beacon, it still has a first-order Fresnel lens in its tower. There's quality tide pooling, an opportunity to visit the sea lions, and a chance to see whales in season here, plus a host of nearby attractions. (See Chapter 43, Santa Cruz Beaches.)

The Santa Cruz Lighthouse testifies to the love two parents had for their son. Now renamed the

Mark Abbott Memorial Lighthouse after its rebuilding in the 1960s, it's the spot to check out the history of local surfing in the shore break or famous "Steamer Lane." There's a collection of paintings of lighthouses past and present, and you're only minutes from the Boardwalk and Wharf. If the surf's up you'll spot hot-dog surfers risking a trip into the rocks below. Otherwise, on a clear day you can see all the way across Monterey Bay to Point Piños Lighthouse in Pacific Grove.

All of these lighthouses work well as stops for a look, a picnic, or a chance to spot whales, seals, sea lions, or sea otters. Kids adore overnight lighthouse stays, and there's a whole series of beaches and parks along Highway 1. Drive down from San Francisco past the Cliff House (note the light on the rocks offshore), stay in or around Santa Cruz, and drive back up the inland route for a wonderful weekend any season of the year.

For more information:

American Youth Hostel, 16 Street, Cabrillo Highway, Montera, CA 94037.

East Brother Light Station, 117 Park Place, Point Richmond, CA 94801, 510-820-9133.

Mark Abbott Memorial (Santa Cruz) Lighthouse, Lighthouse Point, West Cliff Drive, Santa Cruz, CA 95060.

Wine Country and Coast Range

67.

Napa Valley—More than the Wine

There's not much about the Napa Valley that hasn't been said. Robert Louis Stevenson probably said it best in his classic *The Silverado Squatters*. Every travel writer in creation has added a bit, and the TV show *Falcon Crest* polished off any valley mystery. So all I can offer are a few instructions on how, where, and when to avoid the crowds and to look at the old-time valley with minimum exposure to today's crowds and sometimes-tacky tourism. To do this, you need to get away from the big wineries and the most popular tourist spots.

One way to avoid crowds is arrive very, very early in the day, rubberneck before traffic becomes mobbed, and then head toward hills and paths between 9:00 A.M. and 7:00 P.M. Another way is during midweek or off-season visits. Early spring greens the valley nicely, and crowds leave after the fall harvest. A brisk winter day has its points. Another way to enjoy the valley is to stay on the Silverado Trail and laterals or in the foothills, instead of following the main route through St. Helena. Another way that works is "self-propulsion." Hike, bike, horseback ride, and you get out of the exhaust. Such substitutions intensify the pleasures of a visit.

So instead of the Wine Train, with its admittedly decent food and charming, if slow, chug up and back the valley through back yards, consider a bike ride on the Silverado Trail on the uncrowded side of the valley and pack a picnic.

Instead of tours of big wineries such as Christian Brothers, Berringer, or Charles Krug, where you're served by professional greeters, look at Joanne DePuy's California Wine Adventures that take you to special boutique wineries or visit smaller spots such as Stag's Leap, where the owner may pour. If you do this, be prepared to cart cases home. You'll taste wines snapped up before they hit most shops.

Instead of the tourist shops in Yountville's Vintage 1870, where the wine shop, the Chutney Kitchen and Anestis, a fine Greek restaurant across the street deserve some time, browse the Silverado Museum at 1490 Library Lane to see fifteen hundred pieces of Robert Louis Stevenson memorabilia.

Instead of shopping, check out the Bale Grist Mill State Historic Park that once again grinds grain. Tip: Calistoga and St. Helena both offer wonderful baked bread, and just about every spot in the valley sells deli picnic makings.

Instead of a flossy inn or resort, camp at Bothe-Napa Valley State Park and cool off in its swimming pool; instead of another big winery tour, try Bothe-Napa's hiking and riding trails.

Some classics, such as Calistoga's mud baths, are just too good to pass, so plan a couple of hours for a soak in the mud, a massage, or a make-over. Golf or brunch or dinner at the Silverado Country Club deserve time and offer a wonderful round or food in ideal surroundings. The tennis courts are great, too. New offerings include a sail-plane, biplane, and/or balloon rides, or there's the ride up to Sterling Winery. Balloons take off from the Domaine Chandon parking lot near Yountville. The Domaine Chandon is a classic spot to end your day. Call to reserve a table and you'll enjoy some of California's best French food.

Granted, this offers a different look at a favorite valley, but it's a chance to escape, at least for a time, into the valley as it was in its working days.

For more information:
Anestis Grill, 707-944-1500.
Domaine Chandon, 707-944-2892.
State Park Camping, 800-444-7275.
Wine Adventures, Inc., 707-944-8468.

68.

Burbank's Best—The Sonoma Valley

If you must visit in summer, head up to Asti or Healdsburg, check with the Trowbridge folks, and go canoeing for the day. Start early and enjoy the optional barbecue. Then head down to the historic wonders of Sonoma's historic plaza. Take a lunch break at the Toscano Hotel in an Italian restaurant authentic enough to offer extra-virgin olive oil with the exceptional bread. Walk the square, check the shops, and save time for the many other attractions outside of town. For, while most visitors seem to spend a day or a weekend here, it's easy to idle away a week or longer.

Canoe trips on the Russian River have run for nearly fifty years. A number of different runs are available. The best is probably the most upstream run down from Asti. This is, at least in years with reasonable runoff, a reliable option, as upstream releases ensure a good flow. Both Lake Sonoma and Lake Mendocino are great for the fishing, sailing, and camping, but most aquatic types head downstream on the Russian River. Some canoe it with the odd portage all the way down to tidewater at Jenner-by-the-Sea. This is, or mostly was, excellent steelhead water. These days, it's smallmouth bass upstream.

A number of vineyards run along Highway 101, with more, such as Pat Paulson's or the Smothers Brothers', lurking over on Highway 12. But the agricultural heritage of the area is perhaps best exemplified by the incredible collection of produce and fruit available from local stands in season.

In Sonoma proper, history is the name of the day. The northernmost mission, San Francisco Solano de Sonoma, offers a typical Spanish presence enriched by an eight-acre park filled with buildings such as General Vallejo's home or the Depot Park, the Sonoma Barracks, and Sebastiani Indian exhibits that show how the local Coastal Mi-Wok were some of the best basket-makers in America.

There was a large Spanish military presence here as the Russians—before they sold Fort Ross to Captain Sutter—were less than a day's ride away on the coast. In Mexican times, the Bear Flag Revolt established (some might say stole) California as part of the US.

It now seems as if longtime plaza attractions have been there nearly as long—for instance the Sonoma Cheese Company with its famous Sonoma Jack and some rather better, if lesser-known, alternatives that you can sample your way through. But things do change, if slowly. An ice-cream shop becomes a boutique, other shops go gradually upscale, and working artists get priced off square frontage and go to side streets in the usual California pattern.

Some things remain the same. The chance to enjoy lunch under the cool shade of the trees, the sound of a quiet guitar, or the chatter of kids happy at their recent ride down the street on the model trains remain. Hotel rooms with tile floors, Spanish furniture, and plaza views let you stay near the action. It's not far to Glen Ellen and Jack London's Wolf House, and the joys of Napa Valley are just over the hill.

These days, Sonoma might qualify as the far suburbs. It's building more each year, but visitors who tear themselves away from the freeways and visit the neighborhoods, who check out the private gardens, buy lemonade from the kids with a stand, or simply enjoy some of California's most temperate weather open a door to quiet pleasures that haven't quite disappeared from the state.

69.

Coast Range Lake Hideaways

One problem with travel guides is the need for connections. Vacations must be linked so attractions fly one into the other. Activities need to pile up. Thus, smaller spots tend to be overlooked. In part this isn't bad, as small areas tend to become mobbed if they get too much publicity. With this in mind, here's a collection of vest-pocket vacation options on lakes in the Coast Range north of San Francisco. None are on the coast, Highway 1, or Highway 101, so, except for Clear Lake, they're easy to overlook.

Russian Wilderness: The smallest wilderness area in California with only 12 square miles hides near Callahan an hour west of Yreka. It's perfect, but you need to be a skilled backpacker to take advantage of the dozen or so little lakes that hold a batch of small trout. If you like isolation and don't mind bushwhacking, this is the spot.

Trinity Lake: This is the place to go for houseboating if you don't enjoy Lake Shasta's crowds, and it's only a couple of hours to the west.

There's exceptional camping, good ramps, and full-service marinas as well as nice cabins at Cedar Stock Resort. There's an exceptional boater's-only campground at Captain's Point and some excellent fishing for trout and smallmouth bass, if you visit in the spring when the water's up. Unfortunately, Trinity empties fast come summer. Lewiston Lake right below the powerhouse on Trinity Dam also deserves a try.

Blue Lakes: While not as popular as Deer or Bear lakes, there are a flock of Blue Lakes lodges. These are right on Highway 20 between Clear Lake and Highway 101, and nicely fitted out for those who like rustic cabins, modest fishing, and all sorts of resorts, restaurants, camps, and other diverting oddments. All this at budget rates with neither the numbers nor the heat of Clear Lake. If you want to bother with fishing, they do stock trout, but this is more of a getaway spot than most. So take a lake-view cabin, kick back, and let someone else do the cooking and cleaning at prime spots like the Blue Lakes Lodge and Motel or Pine Acres Blue Lakes Resort.

Lake Mendocino: This tidy lake's about eight miles off Highway 101 near Ukiah. An assortment of campgrounds, or Ukiah motels, provide lodging options, and there's a ramp, marina, supplies, and, of course, the famous man-biting catfish. Seems the Fish and Game Department set up some catfish cover and, when the catfish hang out there, they can bite the unwary wader bad enough to leave some welts. Fishing's good here, too, with bass and panfish and a smaller number of planted landlocked striped bass. It's best in spring.

Clear Lake: Okay, it's definitely not a hide-away, but this, the largest natural lake entirely in California, is such a recreational treasure chest that you can't pass it up. While once best known for big bass (and they're coming back), it's the big catfish and all sorts of panfish that make the angling special, and you can hire guides to ensure a decent catch.

However, Clear Lake has lots more to offer than a few fish in and around it's forty-three thousand surface acres. It's a prime water-ski spot—a batch of Aussie pros even come here in the summer to avoid their winter—and there are monthly water-ski contests all summer. Sailing's superb with rental boats, but there's always a sheltered spot to fish—if all else fails, look for these shelters in Clear Lake Oaks Keys.

Homestake Mining Company even has mine tours. This massive mine produces more than two hundred thousand ounces of gold yearly, and more than forty thousand tons of rock are mined each day.

Another prime shoreline diversion is a winery tour. There's a batch of these, with Kendall-Jackson perhaps our favorite and Guenoc running a close second. Low-budget areas like Lake County also attract a mass of those who enjoy crafts. Shopping for pottery, paintings, wood carvings, and jewelry in Lucerne, Nice, or Lakeport is very good and more affordable than in better-known areas.

As a family vacation spot, Clear Lake's hard to beat. Prices are very moderate here, the water's warm, and you'll find pee-wee golf, arcades, paddle boats, golf courses, tennis courts, and more everywhere. It's a bit old-fashioned.

There's history, too, at Anderson Marsh State Historic Park, with its marsh, prehistoric relics, and the more current Anderson Ranch House buildings. Clear Lake State Park, Lake-side County Park, and several public-access areas along the lake's decent frontage roads make access easy. There are more restaurants, shops, and attractions around the lake than you can imagine, and a good number of lodgings offer lake views, fishing piers, or both.

For more information:
Klamath National Forest, 916-842-6131.
Trinity and Lewiston Lakes, 916-623-2121.
Blue Lakes Le Trianon Resort, 707-275-2262.
Pine Acres, 707-275-2811.
Blue Lakes Lodge and Motel, 707-275-2178.
Lake Mendocino, 707-462-7581.
Lake County Chamber of Commerce, 606-263-6131.

70.

Legal Highs—California Ballooning

Ballooning, whether over the Wine Country, the Southern California desert, or Sierras, gets my vote as the best legal high in the state. No other means of transport offers such a chance to see and photograph so much California geography so enjoyably! You can fly all over the state. Most trips float over the Napa-Sonoma wine country, around the San Jose suburbs, above the rice near Davis, over the swimming pools in Palm Springs or San Diego.

From your quiet vantage point aloft, you can hear dogs barking at your balloon's rotund shadow or birds singing in the trees while you vary your altitude from a few feet (almost grape-picking through the vines) to fifteen hundred feet or more, constantly changing your perspective as the wind currents change your course. Then, after your early-morning flight, you enjoy a champagne brunch and other diversions you will treasure for years.

Why not make your next birthday or anniversary even more special? My wife and I certainly did. We rose early to meet the other members of our Napa Valley Balloons, Inc. party at 6:00 A.M. in Yountville, a center for Napa Valley hot-air ballooning. After sorting party members into two separate flights for each of our balloons, we packed into vans for the short trip to the Old Soldiers' Home parking lot, the departure point for our first. Note: The first flight of the day is usually the smoothest, as the air is cool and still. Its only drawback is that you can't take photos of your own balloon taking off and landing. So you might want to leave a spare camera with the ground-support crew.

After the balloon's nylon bag's unrolled, a careful preflight follows. Three massive liquid gas cylinders are loaded into the gondola. Only two cylinders are used in the morning's flights. The third provides a safety backup. Then a powerful portable fan partially inflates the bag, and a careful check is made for tears or other problems. This testing is most reassuring for the first-time "balloonauts."

Once the brightly colored bag bulges off the ground, the propane heater that is held on cables above the gondola fires off with a deep roar. Then, slowly, the bag fills and rises overhead. Passengers clamber aboard over the gondola's high wicker sides to provide needed ballast until liftoff. Wicker, the traditional basket material, still offers a unique combination of strength, light weight, and flexibility.

With a tight hold on the cables, it's time to watch other balloons which sprout like Technicolor mushrooms, then silently rise in the still morning air. The only noise added to dawn's bird calls is the periodic roar of the propane burner that warms the bag's air to carry you aloft. Then, very gently, the ground drops away and you're off. The Soldiers'

Highs over the vineyards

Home recedes into the distance as you soar over green vineyards toward Napa and San Pablo Bay. Once the initial thrill subsided—it never ceases—it's time to watch other balloons, check out the rabbits that race through the vineyard, and keep an eye on the van that holds the second party.

All too soon, it's time to gently set down. Our landing demonstrated our pilot's complete control. We dropped neatly between rows in a vineyard with a foot to spare on each side of the gondola.

Reluctantly, we changed places with the second party—on extra calm days, you might even have three flights. Our ballooning jaunt ended with an al fresco brunch on the grass under the oaks in Yountville's park. First, the pilots recited a special poem to the day's new balloonists. Then came a champagne "christening," and small balloon pins were handed out as treasured mementos of the day's flight. Assorted pastries and breads from splendid local bakeries vied with fresh fruit, cheeses, meats, and much else. They even had a cake for birthday folks such as my wife! A lovely experience, indeed, in the cool of the morning, and it's a perfect way to start a day touring.

For more information:

Napa Valley Balloons, Inc. Yountville, CA 94599, 707-944-0228.

Adventures Aloft Napa Valley, Yountville, CA 94599, 707-255-8688.

Napa's Great Balloon Escape, Napa, CA 94558, 707-253-0800.

71.

Sacramento Locomotion—Steamboats, Railroads, Rafts, and History

Years back, before air conditioning, some Sacramento residents packed up and headed for Tahoe for the summer. Those stuck in town continued to move hoses that kept sprinklers running all summer. Lemonade, rafting on the American River, the heavy shade of huge trees, and the faint breezes on screen porches helped with summer survival. The big California State Fair that runs for more than two weeks through Labor Day celebrates more than the state's massive agricultural presence—it celebrates the onset of cool weather.

Today, Sacramento's much more attractive, and your weekends are considerably cooler. Start a visit with a celebration of autos at the Towe Ford Museum (see Chapter 72, Wheels and Steals). Then move across the parking lot to the California State Railroad Museum, the largest in America. It's on the site where the "Big Four" railroads planned their assault on the Sierra and, perhaps more importantly, that government subsidies made this possible. Railroad owners' creativity deserves a closer examination. Among other things, they convinced the government that the Sierras started twenty-five miles closer to Sacramento than was actually the case. Hence, the Central Pacific got paid for the difficulties of mountain rail laying in alpine venues like Roseville, where they claimed rice used to grow!

With more than a hundred thousand square feet the Rail Museum exhibit spaces are so large it takes most of a day to cover them, especially if you add a seven-mile-long run along the Sacramento River on the Sacramento Southern Excursion Railroad's steam train. Then there's the reconstructed 1876 Central Pacific passenger depot. If you can, read up a bit on railroads so you'll appreciate the wonderful collection of engines and cars.

After all this, it's time for lunch. Old Sacramento, the historic district just behind the levee, deserves a few hours for its old buildings, decent shopping, and quality restaurants where the Pony Express riders wearily dropped off their horses and boarded the sternwheeler to San Francisco. This is also the location of the Sacramento Jazz Festival, which demonstrates the need for additional parking downtown. Check this if you don't mind crowds, heat, and confusion.

Otherwise, you might visit the State Capitol Building, which has been lovingly restored to its gold-capped glory. They used to call it "the Capitol on wheels," for between 1849 and 1855 it moved six times! Tours every hour show you the wonderful detailing of the buildings and its furnishings, what's where, and where you may, on weekdays, see your legislators spending your money. Do spend a quiet moment at the Vietnam Veterans Memorial and remember how freedom comes with a price. Consider a visit to Sutter's Fort—the main building's original, as is the flagpole site. The rest of the fort is a five-eighths scale reconstruction, explaining why the walls look so low, but what can you do when the state only gives you five-eighths of the budget you need. There's a decent American Indian Museum here with one of the best collections of basketry anywhere. It's an open question as to whether Sutter or the Indians lost the most because of the Gold Rush.

If you visit Sacramento during summer, you might want to explore the city one day and spend the next "down the easy river" on a rental raft or canoe over on the American River. Rides leave below Nimbus Dam, with a shuttle bus back to your parking. The water is very calm, and there's no better summer cooler, even in these air-conditioned days, this side of water skiing on the river or at Folsom Reservoir.

Overnights aren't a problem. There's a variety of hotels, a host of campgrounds on the Sacramento and American rivers, and some odd options like the *Delta King,* a hotel that's really a sternwheel steamer, or vice versa.

72.
Wheels and Steals

Automobile museums deserve attention in Northern California, the same as the Behring Auto Museum in the East Bay and the best Ford Museum this side of Dearborn in Sacramento deserve full marks. The last also combines well with a visit to the railroad museum across the street and to Old Sacramento. Best of all, you can get from one museum to the other along some of the best roads in California. Delta drives offer their own rewards (see Chapter 45, The South Delta, and Chapter 73, Delta North).

So whip up, or back, on the freeway, check out one museum, and then leisurely head for the other before or after an overnight in Antioch, Isleton, Locke, or other delightful river towns. Given the choice, drive in the fall when fruit stands offer some of the best pears and produce in California.

Behring Auto Museum: The Behring Auto Museum suits Blackhawk, an upscale East Bay suburb with a massive golf course built by the museum founder. The $12 million granite-and-glass pyramid shouts, rather than hints, of treasures within. The lobby reinforces the "cost is no object" atmosphere, with stainless-steel columns rising to copper-tinted skylights. All this to coddle what most consider the finest collection of one-of-a-kind vehicles in the world—one wag called this "a parking lot for *The Rich and Famous!*" Too bad politics and personalities have tossed mud on the museum's windows.

Like old-time movie stars? Check Rudolph Valentino's 1926 Isotta Fraschini or Clark Gable's 1935 Dusenberg convertible coupe. Royalty suit your tastes? HRH Queen Mary's 1955 Daimler, the Aga Khan's 1952 Rolls-Royce Phantom IV Sedanca, or the Shah of Iran's 1939 Bugatti Cabriolet deserve a good look.

Favor lame ducks? Check the 1958 Edsel Citation convertible described as "one of the worst mistakes in the history of the auto industry." The Tucker 48, once called "the car of tomorrow—today," set the auto world buzzing back in 1948 with its swiveling light, fuel injection, and aerodynamic styling. These and about one hundred of the vehicles in the two-hundred-and-thirty-vehicle collection are displayed on the "budget" ground floor, where most car values run from $500,000 to $750,000.

However, for the car buff, Andre Dubonnet's 1924 Hispano-Suiza Racer, called the "Hope Diamond of Automobiles," is the prize, valued at $4.5 million. That's pretty dear for a wooden car, until you see its varnished tulipwood body with thousands of brass rivets and copper trim, and wheel spokes that impress even the most die-hard "econo-box" owner.

Dubonnet's classic revolves on a special platform on the second floor of the museum where vehicles worth over $1 million each are displayed. As elsewhere in the museum, there are no railings, glass cases, or ropes. So those who take the guided tours can closely examine each classic up close.

In addition to the $100-million collection of cars, the museum's Antiques Resource Library holds more than thirty tons of books, catalogs, press clippings, and photographs about classic automobiles since 1960. It was compiled by Wellington Everett Miller, a famous custom coachworker. An adjunct of the University of California, the Behring Auto Museum shows what you can collect with an unlimited budget and either good taste or good advice.

Towe Ford Museum: A rather ugly warehouse building on Sacramento's Front Street next to the river holds one of the most complete collections of Fords in the world. Cars are sometimes less than mint and a bit jammed in, but that's not unusual where the collection is so huge. It's worth a visit, because you can see examples of every year and model Ford made between 1903 and 1953! Even allowing for the duration of the Model T and A, this represents a major collecting effort.

If possible, visit on the weekend, when the parking lot across from the entrance is the site of a great many classic-car club meetings. Nearby, Old Sacramento's California State Railroad Museum steam trains, the steamer *Delta King*, and the B.F. Hastings Building, the western end of the Pony Express back before California went car crazy, can fill out the day.

For more information:

The Behring Auto Museum, 3750 Blackhawk Plaza Circle, Danville, CA 94526, 415-736-2277.

Towe Ford Museum, 2200 Front Street, Sacramento, CA 95818, 916-442-6802.

73.

Delta North

From space, the glistening spider web of the California delta funnels down to the Carquinez Straits, where it punches through the hills to the bay and ocean. But this is temporary. When the mountain men followed the beavers west, they found a vast marsh in the great central valley of

California. Rivers ran free and, in the spring, spread out across the valley that bloomed under this natural irrigation.

Today, the rivers are trapped behind dams and, in the delta, levees, but the rivers always win. Each year, inches of the fertile but friable peat soil blow away. And also each year, the water pressure on the fragile levees, built mostly by Chinese labor after the railroads hooked up at Promontory Point, increases. It's just a matter of time until the levees go. So enjoy the delta now. Go by houseboat, drive the roads, and try the ferries. It's unlikely that it would be rebuilt if the massive outer levees ever went from a combination of floods, high tides, and strong winds.

The North Delta, which is all the ground and water north of a line drawn across from the Martinez Bridge to the Sierra, offers more traffic than the South (see Chapter 45, The South Delta). It's more accessible, too, but still a good place to go for a quiet, probably aquatic vacation that allows you to watch the water and the shore from a resort, campground, or houseboat. As a low-pressure choice, the delta's ideal for recharging batteries if you pick a section to match your needs.

Wind subdivides the delta. The windy West Delta runs from the mothball fleet by the Martinez Bridge up the Sacramento River to Rio Vista and over to Sherman Lake and Frank's Track. So houseboat rentals in this area run to seaworthy displacement hulls rather than the dual pontoons usual elsewhere. Windy Rio Vista does offer solid conditions, and a school to learn wind surfing. It's also a wild spot in the summer when the water skiers gang up here, with wet T-shirt and bikini contests, personal watercraft, and the numbers of the hard-body set peaking. The Sacramento

River side of the delta definitely has the best fishing, too.

The San Joaquin River noses in to join with the Sacramento River near here. It's not unusual to see big container ships in either river, and they have the right of way as they can't leave the dredged channel—"ragbaggers" take note.

Just south of Twitchell Island, the Mokelumne River's North Fork puts clean water into the East Delta. It's a dandy spot to swim or ski, and it's accessible from Highway 12, which runs east to west from Rio Vista over to Interstate 5. This section of the delta seems a quieter, gentler place unless you moor up in the Meadows on a weekend when the party hearty types zoom in. Otherwise, it's easy to find an isolated, sheltered spot to anchor.

Boats are the best way to get to parts of the delta that drivers never see, and you can rent them everywhere. Bethel Island's a good starting point, with the biggest concentration of houseboat rentals in the delta. If you own a boat, launching's easy at Brannon Island and a number of other spots. Brannon Island State Recreation Area has nice improved campgrounds, too.

If you can't, or won't, boat, you can start your delta explorations by crossing the Antioch Bridge to the north and running along the Sacramento River all the way through Isleton and it's crawdad-crazed residents to Walnut Grove's wonderful pear orchards. Isleton goes crawdad crazy in June, when more than a hundred thousand visitors flood in for the three-day festival, but it's a nice stop for dinner or for picnic makings, with particularly good local sausage and wonderful fruit in season. The old Chinatown section is upscaling with bookstores and restaurants, as well; you can even buy croissants.

Then it's just a quick zip on to Locke, the only rural Chinese town in America, and its modest museum, and, in the summer, more interesting community gardens that grow a variety of Oriental vegetables. The wooden buildings and stores survived, but the original residents worked their way up the economic ladder and out of town.

The levee road continues on up to Courtland and all the way to Sacramento. It's a scenic, quiet, and rather slow route that does pay off with wonderful produce stands, and in spring, there's dandy blackberry picking along every river. Aside from the river roads and Highway 12, driving in the deltas tests your map reading. Drawbridges make life interesting. So do ferries to Steamboat and Cache Sloughs that are made up of remnant populations of many ferries past. Most delta bridges replaced ferries and often carried on their name. You will notice different types of bridges—the Rio Vista Bridge is a lift type, and most of the rest are bascule-bridges, which use a heavy weight at one end to counterbalance the weight of the roadway so that quite a small motor can swing it up.

For more information:
Bethel Island, 510-684-2260.
Brannon Island State Recreation Area, 916-777-6671.
Isleton Chamber of Commerce, 916-777-5880.

74.

The Three, or More, Shastas

From the outlook above the Sacramento River, you can see the three Shastas: the dam, the lake, and the 14,162-foot mountain. These only open the game for visitors. Add Mount Lassen, which is still active, the Trinity Alps, and the California end of the Cascade Mountains, plus seven national forests and eight national and state parks.

Their sum is a vacation destination that's the least crowded in California. It's just a zip up Interstate 5.

The popular place to start is Lake Shasta with its caverns, 365 miles of shoreline, dozens of resorts and campgrounds, and hundreds of houseboats. During summer, each and every cove fills with moored houseboats, and water-skiers zip here, there, and everywhere. It's a time for splashing fun and dodging the snags in the Pit River Arm, and it's a time to cool off with a visit to Shasta Caverns. Visit in the spring, when the dam spillway's wet and your views max out with the greening of Shasta. In the fall, you find the lake levels down, the trees turned gold, and the banks brown and bare, but, as in spring, you'll enjoy off-season rates, superior fishing, and relative isolation. Thanksgiving or Christmas holiday houseboat trips offer unique rewards for those heroic enough to brave the chance of cold weather—we found you can even cook a sixteen-pound turkey in the on-board oven.

It's easy to escape Lake Shasta crowds. Head in any direction. To the west, the mountains of the Trinity and Klamath offer some of the least-crowded backpacking in the state (see Chapter 69, Coast Range Lake Hideaways), and if you do not mind roads that wind and wind and wind, there's some splendid driving down the Trinity River Scenic Byway. Farther west and north, the Marble Mountains add their trails. Weaverville—stop and check out the Historic Joss House—opens the winding road to the coast, and the Klamath River hides some dandy raft and kayak days accessible with a host of white-water and steelhead guides and much more.

To the south, consider time on the Sacramento River. You can boat or float from the Red Bluff Diversion Dam all the way downstream to

Sacramento or even San Francisco if you are ambitious and pick a calm bay day. We canoed this in our salad days and found plenty of shoreline campgrounds, a host of riparian habitat, and more mosquitoes than you can count. These days, the banks of the river are riprapped downstream in the delta so that the best run is from Red Bluff down to Colusa's State Recreation Area just off Highway 20. If you fish for fall salmon and steelhead runs or try for trout year-round, do not forget that bass are available and often overlooked.

North of Shasta, the canyon narrows down to pinch in the Upper Sacramento River, Interstate 5, and the railroad. A massive chemical spill damaged this section of the river, but it's been restored to pristine condition and seems more appreciated than ever by locals and visitors alike for its fine trout fishing.

The McCloud River, off Highway 44 toward Fall River Mills, offers incredible fishing waters, lovely trees, and vistas of Mount Shasta and Lassen. Look for camping here and along Hat Creek. Continue on and the highway dumps you out into the upper fringes of Mount Lassen where, if you simply follow the Lassen Scenic Byway, turning right at the lava, you can run a ring around Lassen. Mount Lassen offers the smelly delights of active volcanic areas plus a decorative, if distorted, assortment of lava and cinder cones and beds (see Chapter 88, Eagle Lake—Ospreys and Isolation).

The Lassen Scenic Byway runs back toward Chester and Lake Almanor. Take the short detour into Westwood and try the homemade pie at the cafe. Almanor's got good fishing, decent boating, and relatively easy access to Lassen. Then it's a choice of routes back home via Red Bluff to Interstate 5 or past Honey Lake to Truckee or Reno.

For more information:
Shasta-Cascade Wonderland Association, 800-326-6944.
Colusa-Sacramento State Recreation Area, 916-458-4927.

75.

All the Way to Alturas

Ecologically speaking, Alturas is part of the Great Basin, not California. It comes as close to splendid isolation as any place in the Golden State. It's easier to drive the hundred and seventy-six miles there from Reno or the ninety-seven miles from Oregon's Klamath Falls than the winding hundred and forty-seven miles from Redding. This simply isn't a weekend stop, unless you like to drive more hours than you recreate, but it's ideal for longer visits, possibly in conjunction with visits to Mount Lassen or Reno. Once you arrive, you'll know the trip is worth it.

Isolation left Alturas in a time warp that's best appreciated with a one-and-a-half-mile walk through town that starts with the Modoc County Museum where you can pick up a guidebook. This seems a nice way to work out the kinks after the long drive. Killer Kane's Bar, the Niles Saloon and High Grade Room, and the Hole-in-the-Wall Saloon suggest things were lively in the past. Other highlights of the walk include a number of fine brick and cut-stone buildings such as the depot of the Nevada, California & Oregon Railroad and its office building that's now an Elks Lodge.

The high-plains country around Alturas runs to big sky and open vistas—it's no accident that one of the popular reservoirs is called "Big Sage." All this space and a wild, winding, and usually unmarked network of dirt roads makes this 4WD heaven. So do a very large number of unattractive to downright ugly reservoirs that lack improved camping, shade trees, and scenery, but in the case of Dorris, Ballared, and most others, hold big trout. With so many choices, if you don't catch fish reasonably soon, head somewhere else.

All of these reservoirs also offer wonderful bird- and wildlife-watching as there's not a lot of other water in the high plains. You'll spot waterfowl, antelope, wild horses, mule deer, and much else. Most of all, they offer an old-style kind of camping without the regimentation of most improved camps. Do, of course, pack out what you bring in. A lot of the best spots offer neither garbage cans nor collection.

Drivers find their own joys here. You actually can explore with the aid of a Modoc National Forest map and find reservoirs and lakes where you'll be the only visitor. You don't have to fish to enjoy this country, but you do have to like isolation, quiet, and an open sense of space that's just about disappeared in the rest of California.

It's not usual but, during cooler months, mountain bikers can do wonderfully well on the many dirt roads and open trails. If you backpack and have not tried the South Warner Wilderness Area, you've a treat worth the day-long ride.

Frankly, if I'd not moved out of range of these mountains, I'd never mention them. Ecologically, they divide in half at the crest. The west side runs to pines and streams and is our choice for camps. The Great Basin side's sage, much like Nevada, with not much besides sage to block views or snag backcasts. The way to see this is from the Summit Trail, a twenty-four-mile hike that's moderately demanding over two days, but a nice four- or five-day trip that allows hikers to check out a half dozen lakes and streams. Nope, you've got to find your own spots to fish. As a rule, you'll do best with lakes and stream sections a bit off the trail.

Most of all, you'll do best if you like your own company, can paddle your own canoe, light your own fires, fix your own flats, and enjoy the sense of space and self-sufficiency you find when you, as the Aussies say, "go walk around in the bush."

For more information:

Alturas Chamber of Commerce, 916-233-4434.

Modoc National Forest, 916-233-4611.

The North Coast

76.

Happy in Humboldt— Eureka, Klamath, and More

Prairie Creek Redwoods State Park may offer the nicest camping in the redwoods. Arcata has a fine university. Add a chain of lagoons, a wonderful bay, the Victorian homes of Eureka, the Azalea State Reserve, and more elk, deer, birds, and shore action than anyone needs. The result could only be Humboldt County, and it's a very good thing indeed that it's a full day's drive north from the Bay area, or it would be overwhelmed with tourists.

Wise visitors head all the way to the Oregon border and the killer camping in Prairie Creek, because if you start at the south end of the county, you'll never make it up north. A whole series of fresh-water lagoons, with surf fishing on the ocean side, run down to Patrick's Point State Park and Trinidad Harbor. A short visit to Lady Bird Johnson Grove and the other virgin redwoods offers the best viewing on the Coast. Fern Canyon's another good spot to see both redwoods and the elk that wander there.

Trinidad Head, its trails, and the Memorial Lighthouse replica in town are worth a look, and the Trinidad Museum offers a decent overview. Don't miss the boats, clamming, musseling, and a chance for some world-class berry picking.

Just inland, you'll escape the fog in Willow Creek on the Trinity Scenic Byway and Trinity River. Rafting, kayaking, and lots of up-and-down hiking in heavily wooded "Big Foot" country increase your options. The Hoopa Village is the largest reservation in California and perhaps the nicest chance to visit Native Americans. The tribal museum and seasonal American Indian Days deserve a look.

Humboldt Bay is the population center of the county, and Eureka, the county seat, needs at least a day or two on its own. Old Town Eureka Victorians are typified by the most photographed Victorian home in America, the Carson Mansion, at Second and M Streets. Unfortunately, it's not open to the public. But there are enough other Old Town Victorian shops to fill a couple of hours, and the Chamber of Commerce suggests a nice walking tour. A working Victorian molding mill, a park and zoo, the Romano Gabriel Sculpture Garden—don't miss this folk art marvel—and Fort Humboldt with its vintage logging exhibit can take the rest of the day even if you don't head south to the Humboldt Bay National Wildlife Refuge to see the shore birds, seals, and such.

You can get a closer look with the Humboldt Bay Harbor Cruise on the *Madaket,* a 1910 ferry that's a State Historic Vessel and takes about seventy-five minutes. There's also the North Coast Railroad if you'd rather not leave the tracks.

Lodgings can be Victorian, too. An elegant Victorian mansion specializes in pampering, the Tudor delights of the Eureka Inn offer visual rewards, you'll find a host of b and bs and the usual chain motels.

Food's good here. There's everything from cafe to continental food. The Samoa Cookhouse with its loggers' meals is a solid option; so are the many seafood houses along the docks such as Lazio's, which has been there since the 1880s, or Weatherby's, a newcomer established in 1946.

Then it's time for live theater at North Coast Rep or Plays in Progress. The Redwood Ballet offers the *Nutcracker*, at Christmas, and then there's the Eureka Symphony Orchestra. There are advantages of visiting spots near college communities like Arcata. Humboldt State University has all the usual attractions, and the town supplies customers with some nifty restaurants and sidewalk cafes. Just outside town, Arcata Marsh offers incredible birding plus a choice of trails to bike and hike. If it's been years since you were part of campus life, there's no better place for a little hand-holding than over an espresso in a dime coffee house.

After a day or two in Eureka, head back on the road (see Chapter 77, Ferndale—Out of the Way Exceptional). The Avenue of the Giants deserves a day of its own. Most visitors make the mistake of whipping through on the lateral off Highway 101. It takes more time than that for the redwoods to imbue their sense and scent. Drive down the massive avenue, find a spot to stop, park, and walk away from the pavement until you can't hear the traffic. Then sit on a log and close your eyes. Smell the trees. Listen to the birds. Open your eyes and imagine a time before roads. It's as close as you can come to an out-of-body experience without chemical enhancement. Then it's time for a picnic and the long ride home.

For more information:

Humboldt County Convention and Visitors Bureau, 800-346-3482.

Eureka Chamber of Commerce, 800-442-3738.

Willow Creek Chamber of Commerce, 916-629-2693.

77.

Ferndale—Out of the Way Exceptional

Ferndale combines kooky and country. Consider its history as a dairy town where Victorian "Buttermilk Palaces" testify to the tons of milk and cheese shipped south to San Francisco. Factor in the scenic delights of the nearby Avenue of the Giants, where redwoods left standing from former logging days offer a chance for an aching neck as you crane upward in wonder. Factor in a nice little beach without crowds, the Eel River with its steelhead and kayaking, and a nearby college town. Shake everything up with an earthquake or three and perhaps the strangest "race" in America, and you have a destination worth the rather long drive up Highway 101 from the Bay area.

Ferndale's main street, with its classic Victorian buildings, working artists, and better food than anyone has the right to expect in an old, out-of-the-way small town, deserves a half day on its own. Consider it a Mendocino or Carmel without tourists—think of time, rather than distance—and it is about as far from San Francisco today as Carmel was in the bohemian days between the wars. You do not find T-shirts. You do find wonderful art and some of the most affordable wood carvings and pottery anywhere. An artists' co-op and with individual ateliers, you watch art as it's created.

In between the artisans and artists, you can help support the local dairy industry with samples of homemade ice cream and candy. Leave room for dinner at the hotel—it's a wonderful chance to try seafood dishes made from fresh-caught mussels or clams from nearby local waters. The hotel offers Victorian rooms at a moderate price. Just off Main

Street, the Gingerbread Mansion Bed and Breakfast has, among other foibles, a room with his and her clawfoot tubs—reservations are recommended. There is even an inexpensive motel and useful, although rather ugly, campsites at the fairgrounds.

Just out of town, Russ Park, a small park with redwoods, provides a chance to walk off dinner, but the beach deserves more time. Just watch for sneaker waves if you make it down to the water. You will doubtless see a collection of shore birds and may spot seals or sea lions.

Given the hideaway location just minutes off Highway 101, only the depraved or demented would visit on Memorial Day weekend, when the Arcata-to-Ferndale Kinetic Sculpture Race is in full swing. It's three days of foolishness over bay, mudflats, and beach, with contraptions that live up to names like Rickety Chickadee or Tyrannosaurus Rust. If they do not sink before they finish, you will spot survivors of previous races in their namesake museum on Ferndale's Main Street.

Other local attractions include State Route 211, the long, winding, slow road down through Capetown, Petrolia, and Honeydew along the Matole River. This offers the most uncrowded view of the California coast all the way down to Shelter Cove and serves as an excellent alternative to Highway 101. There's a demanding Tour of the Unknown Coast Bicycle Race on this road, but it's a better slow and scenic tour with rubbernecking stops.

Nice area. Few crowds. Cool shore. Good grub. Decent lodging. 'Nuff said.

For more information:
Ferndale Chamber of Commerce, 707-786-4477.

78.

Northern California Light Housekeeping

There's a special air about lighthouses and their often associated foghorns that only those who went to sea before radar, Loran, and global-positioning devices know. I barely made this period, but when my uncles and I needed to get back through the Golden Gate, we listened hard. You couldn't see the lights in heavy fog, but you could listen, and with some local knowledge, we could listen our way in under the horn that still honks from its perch on the middle of the Golden Gate Bridge.

Lighthouses started early in California. The Pacific isn't always that peaceful, and the combination of fog and rocky coasts caused early explorers to miss the Golden Gate bites. By the 1850s, transplanted Cape Cod buildings with a light tower in their center sprang up on Battery Point, Point Arena, Point Reyes, East Brothers, Point Montera, Pigeon Point, and Santa Cruz on the Northern California Coast. Pacific Grove has a lighthouse that was run by women for forty years (see Chapter 40, Pacific Grove).

Today, artists and photographers swarm about lighthouses and, if you plan a weekend carefully, you can visit all the lighthouses on the North Coast except the East Brothers Light in San Francisco Bay. It deserves a special trip of its own. The restored 1873 lighthouse is a nonprofit b and b with a 360-degree view and the most romantic overnight imaginable. Call or write way ahead, as it's only open Thursday through Sunday.

For the rest of the tourists, you need to combine lighthouse visits with other activities. Point Reyes works well with a look at the whales, a visit to the

Light house keeping

National Seashore, and something like clamming if you're fit enough to manage the three hundred steps. Since the lighthouse is on top of a 580-foot cliff, it's a splendid outlook for gray-whale migrations and is a birder's favorite.

The next visit north is Point Arena Lighthouse, the first steel-reinforced concrete lighthouse in the US—done after the first lighthouse didn't survive the 1906 earthquake. There's a decent museum with some dandy early photos, lovely meadows nearby, and more. If you plan to stay overnight in the area, check the three rental homes in the vicinity.

Farthest north of our notable lighthouses is Battery Point in Crescent City. It's a tricky visit, as you need to hike across at low tide, but it beats the steps at Point Reyes! There's some splendid clamming nearby. The associated museum isn't bad, either.

These last two lighthouses belong on the home leg of a weekend or long weekend trip that would range up through the redwood country on Highway 101 to Crescent City and then meander back through Point Reyes, Mendocino, Tomales Bay, and on down past the reconstructed Russian fort in Fort Ross, and past Benicia and Stinson Beach.

For more information:

East Brothers Light Station, 117 Park Place, Point Richmond, CA 94801, 510-820-9133.

Point Arena Lighthouse Keepers, Inc., Box 11, Point Arena, CA 95468.

Point Reyes Lighthouse, Point Reyes National Seashore, Point Reyes, CA 94956.

79.

California's Lost Coast

The first oil strike in California was way back in 1861 in Petrolia on the Mattole River near Cape Mendocino, the westernmost point in California, and it's a good thing the oil ran out fast. Not much has happened since it did and since the loggers left. So if you're adventurous enough to bushwhack back into the King Range National Conservation Area on your way to the Sinkyone Wilderness Area, an almost entirely overlooked coastal treasure, California's Lost Coast could be for you. Tip: Drive in past Well's Gold School on Bear Harbor Road, not on the awful road through White Thorn.

There's also a mild-version visit. Shelter Cove, a coastal hideaway of the fiscally secure, offers homes for lease, a wonderful set of tiny beaches, rocky shorelines, and enough supplies to keep you going. There's even an airstrip for the fly-in folks with more money than time. But the best part of the area, the real, working part of the area, runs down the Mattole Valley and its namesake river, where the steelhead still run. Add some cockle clamming, outstanding rock fishing, and a choice of hikes, rides, and, most beautiful of all, beach or redwoods backpacking trips, and you can see a part of California that has not entered the twentieth century.

The Mattole River Resort is popular with anglers and others who appreciate the five rustic housekeeping cabins eighty feet above the Mattole River and above the fog and rain. It's not too far from Honeydew or the Petrolia Bar & Grill—a short drive along Lighthouse Road to the Lost Coast Beach that runs south to provide an unusual three-day beach hike to Shelter Cove.

The road continues past Petrolia an hour or so on toward Ferndale, if you can pass the temptation of interesting lateral roads and trails down to a seven-mile-long beach. Some of the beaches along this section of the coast are open and exciting for 4WD. Many others, like those to the south, are closed. So it's important to read regulations, and it's prudent to have a means of getting unstuck. The nearest tow truck is probably a couple of hundred dollars away.

All this is part of the King Range National Conservation Area and the Sinkyone Wilderness area with its sixty thousand acres of steep, wet, and wonderful woods. If you visit, go in the summer, as the October to April winter season averages a hundred inches of rain a year and two hundred inches or more in wet years. You'll find a totally unique experience and a wonderfully cool summer vacation.

For more information:

BLM (for King Range information), 707-442-1721.

Mattole River Resort, 800-845-4607

Shelter Cove Information Bureau, 707-986-7609

The Foothills

80.

Highway 49 North

The "Northern Mines" is the proper term for the northern end of the chain of gold towns built at the lower edge of the snow line. These charming towns run from just north of Jacksonville through Placerville and the John Marshall Gold Discovery State Park on the American River. Then they wind up the hill to Auburn and its Old Town before heading into Grass Valley and Nevada City (see Chapter 82, Progress and Preservation in Grass Valley and Nevada City) and then past a site near the Yuba River where Black Bart once held up the stage. Continue on to the Gold Lakes Basin and Sierra City and, partner, "you've come to the end of the trail." Well, at least the end of Highway 49.

Since this section of the Sierra foothills lurks close to Sacramento, the best time to visit is doubtless spring or just after fall rains. Frankly, this seems an area best toured as part of your own personal search for a place where you hole up and avoid the tourist crush. Some do this with bed and breakfasts or resorts just off Highway 49. Others head up into pointy-tree country in Ebbetts or Donner Pass. Some hide on houseboats. More than a few visitors seem to enjoy the hustle and bustle of crowds and confusion.

More solitary types find that weekends in the summer tend to crowd one out; winter finds lots of traffic up and over Ebbetts, Donner, and other passes to snow country. It's also wise to consider the commuter traffic between Jackson and Grass Valley.

Start early, or drive during the middle of the day, and you'll find fewer vehicles sharing the generally winding two-lane road.

Sutter Creek just up Highway 49 from Jackson offers a batch of antiques shops and side trips to Volcano or Pine Grove's Indian Grinding Rock State Historic Park.

Placerville, once called "Hangtown" for the rather draconian local justice system, runs to Gold Bug Mine Park and a couple of decent museums.

It's not much farther on to the two-hundred-acre Marshall Gold Discovery State Historic Park, where there's a replica of Captain Sutter's sawmill, the millrace that produced James Marshall's gold nuggets that set off the Gold Rush. Several rafting outfitters run from here down to Folsom Reservoir, Sacramento's backyard impoundment.

The highway winds along the river and up the hill overlooking what appears to be a never-to-be-completed site of the Auburn Dam. There's interesting fishing upstream and down here. Grind up the hill and you're in Auburn and the Old Town just off Interstate 80. The oldest post office and volunteer fire department in the West are here. A number of other buildings sprawl off the freeway in a sort of wishbone. Those who whiz by on Interstate 80 miss decent antiques shops and at least a half dozen restaurants.

With as limited contact with the Interstate as you can manage, it's on to Grass Valley and Nevada City. There's a nice little reservoir, Rollins Lake, that few visitors find. It's best in the spring. With time spent in Grass Valley and Nevada City, next head on over the Middle Fork of the Yuba River. This is a popular, if sometimes dangerous, swimming area with locals. Note: There's a nice side road down to Bullards Bar just after you cross over the

North Fork of the Yuba River. The campground here is a little noisy—trucks downshift as they round the rock where Black Bart once held up the Wells Fargo Stage—but you have a chain of campgrounds all the way to Downieville and Sierra City.

The road's an excellent spot to watch the rafters or, in season, the divers who run gold dredges along the river. Those who work hard can make an ounce or so of gold a day, so it's a popular and well-regulated summer activity. Tip: Local trout find a free lunch off the back end of the dredges and soon gather when the diving miners fire up their dredges.

For more information:
Grass Valley Chamber of Commerce, 916-273-4667.
Nevada City Chamber of Commerce, 916-265-2692.

81.

Progress and Preservation in Grass Valley and Nevada City

A local wit calls Grass Valley and Nevada City "two towns separated by a minimum altitude and maximum attitude." Both gained golden fame. Grass Valley, with the hard-rock gleanings of Cornish miners who drove three hundred and sixty-six miles of tunnels, sports the Empire Mine, now a historic park, but elected to point with pride toward progress. Nevada City retains more of a fly-in-amber attitude with its historic gaslit Main Street.

Visitors enjoy both towns. Grass Valley's Empire Mine is particularly nice in the spring when the roses bloom, and the Nevada County Museum on Lower Mill Street has a couple of floors of mining equipment and a model of the stamp mills that once pounded rocks to powder and gold. The mine tour's particularly recommended with its manor house and a vast assortment of necessary outbuildings. Helpful docents show you where they once took out nearly $6 million worth of gold.

Drive down Lower Mill Street toward town, and you'll pass the Chamber of Commerce in what was once the home of Lola Montez. She deserves consideration if only as the one-time lover of mad Kind Ludwig of Bavaria, who, among other things, built the only one-bedroom castle. "What Lola wants, Lola gets" certainly applied here as, among other foibles, Lola kept a pet bear. She also taught her trades to Lotta Crabtree, a local girl, who became a celebrated star of the late 1800s.

Grass Valley offers nifty steaks at the Owl Cabins and some dandy baked goods, plus the chance to sample a Cornish pasty, traditional meat pies in pastry that miners took down into the tunnels and heated with their lamps. Tip: A splash of malt vinegar's traditional on the pasties, and you can buy them next door to the old library.

Check into the local mystery of flight. It's claimed by some that Lyman Gilmore flew an aircraft here before the Wrights. Locals apparently agreed enough to name a school for their "pre-historic" airman. The library has details.

Downhill from Grass Valley in Penn Valley toward Marysville, there's a wonderful covered bridge on the South Fork of the Yuba River; follow the signs past Lake Wildwood. Golfers find Lake Wildwood's eighteen-hole course one of the best in California if they can figure how to get in past the gate guards.

The deep, clear pools just downstream from the bridge seem a popular spot to swim. You also can pan for gold or hike down the bank a half mile to Lake Englebright, a nifty reservoir with boater's-only campgrounds. Continue on and you reach Highway 49 and the back route into Nevada City.

Nevada City retains its old-time atmosphere at the price of limited parking and a certain smug sense of self that's probably deserved. Park over by the American Victorian Museum on Broad Street and check out the furniture and the teddy bears—there's even a teddy bear convention here. Walk a block up to Main Street and plan on spending a couple of hours in the ten or so bookstores, the mining shop that offers panning lessons, and some very upscale clothing outlets. There's a dandy theater that runs to everything from flamenco and melodrama to classical music. It's the oldest in California, and Mark Twain appeared here.

Firehouses—one's now the Nevada City Museum—deserve a look, and you can take a self-guided tour with a map from the Chamber of Commerce, which is down at the bottom of the hill in the oldest building in town, the one with a stamp mill out front. Or you can opt for a couple of hours of a guided tour or a short carriage drive around town.

As a rule, it's best to park near the creek at the bottom of the hill, head up one side of Main, and when you're tired, chug back down the other. Broad Street and Pine offer plenty of neat spots to stop, rest the feet, and enjoy a cup of coffee. If you extend your visit until dinner, the wonderful European food at Selaya's is worth the price. Try the duck and seasonal fresh fish. Note: There's a pre-theater dinner package, and reservations are a must.

Lodgings range from some of the best b and bs in town to the historic National Hotel on Broad Street. Grandmere's Inn, on the National Register of Historic Places, is a good choice in Nevada City. So is the old Holbrooke House in Grass Valley. A number of campgrounds offer low-cost stays toward Downieville or Interstate 80.

Options don't stop here. Malakoff Diggins State Park and North Bloomfield show why California was the first state to ban hydraulic mining that denuded and sent mud down the hills. It's a nice spot to picnic. Drivers can wind back into the Sierras and follow dirt roads, most sans signs, all the way over the Sierras to Truckee. At least forty lakes and reservoirs wait for 4WD types or hikers, and there's a small wilderness area as well.

Bullards Bar Reservoir has boating, rental houseboats, drive-in camps, and decent trout and bass fishing just a few miles off Highway 49. The Bear River, all three forks of the Yuba River (see Chapter 81, Highway 49 North) deserve a look. You also can raft on the North Fork in spring. Check the often-overlooked country around North San Juan, where you can still find a remnant population of hippies, or visit Washington with its miners and, rumor has it, nude swimming hole on the North Fork of the Yuba.

Part of a conversation overheard in the local laundromat between two sandaled, long-skirted ladies with graying hair: "Where did we go wrong with Lysander? We home-schooled him, and now he's got a scholarship to Harvard and he wants to be a tax lawyer. He's even eating meat!"

During winter, and especially during December when Cornish Christmas, Museum Open House, theater, music, and more remind the bookish of Dickens, there's no better place to vacation. You're in just enough snow to dust the trees, an hour from fine skiing, and an easy drive from the Bay Area.

For more information:

Grass Valley Chamber of Commerce, 916-273-4667.

Nevada City Chamber of Commerce, 916-265-2692.
Empire Mine State Historic Park, 916-273-8522.
Selaya's Restaurant, 916-265-5697.

82.

Camping Considered

Resorts, RVs, and day trips have their virtues, but only camping—or its self-propelled variation, backpacking—let you listen to the wind in the trees, watch the moonlight, smell the pines, and, yes, find out why you neither pitch tents in holes nor leave the Off or mosquito netting home. Nothing tastes better than food cooked and eaten in the open, and while the experience may be a one-time-only-thing, like skydiving, it's something all kids, and all but the most coddled adults, should try.

California camping runs the gambit from the winter desert, fall foothill, summer redwood country, or even the county park just a few miles from home.

Gearing up's easy. Most mountain shops that sell camping gear rent it, or you can ease into tenting with a rental in Yosemite, a wall tent at Packer Lake, or any of a number of other spots that offer wall tents and such. You might try a combination day-and-night outing and opt for a raft trip with an overnight stay or let a horse packer take you back into the mountains. Own a boat? You can tote more than you think to wonderful shore campgrounds on most California reservoirs—the best of these may be in Emerald Bay on Lake Tahoe.

Gear need not be extensive in mild weather. Something soft, such as an air mattress and a set of folded blankets, does the job, and you only need a tent if bugs or rain intrude on your pleasures. If you want to buy, you can save a bundle with garage-sale Coleman gear and the like.

Where to go isn't a problem. Try short, overnight vacations for a start and then move on to longer trips. In Northern California, you'll find prime camping in the Muir Woods and a number of delta sites. Add most foothill reservoirs and a string of campgrounds that follow Highway 1.

It's a different vacation, an old-fashioned vacation, and a vacation that too many miss. It's also the least expensive vacation option after staying with relatives. Then, too, if you don't like it, you don't have to tough out the weekend. As we noted in our snow-survival classes, the best survival gear when a blizzard blows in is the combination of a car key and a motel.

For more information:
Grass Valley Chamber of Commerce, 916-273-4667.
Nevada City Chamber of Commerce, 916-265-2692.

83.

Sierra Low Down—Twain Harte et al

Early settlers in California were smart when they settled in the foothills below the snow, but above most of the valley heat. These days, those who seek the Sierras have not learned this lesson, and most head up into pointy-tree country above four thousand feet. The visitors who do stay in the foothills spend their time on and around Highway 49. Everyone's favorite foothill highway does offer a history lesson everyone should see at least once, but if you seek a bit more isolation a bit closer than the

Sierra peaks, try foothill towns like Twain Harte off Highway 49.

Twain Harte lurks just eleven miles up the hill on Highway 108 from Sonora. Any town named after Mark Twain and Bret Harte (like Steinbeck and Norris, must-read authors for any California traveler), gets a head start. It worked that way for a time when the town was Twain Harte Resort in 1924, and it took ten hours to drive over from the Bay area.

These days, Twain Harte is perhaps more popular as a retirement area than a resort, and most Highway 108 visitors whiz past in their haste to get up the hill to Pinecrest or Dodge Ridge Ski Area. But Twain Harte is so modestly priced, so conveniently located, and so lovingly cared for that, like Murphy's and other Gold Country towns off the main tourist track of Highway 49, it's a solid choice for a weekend or longer stay.

Getting there from the Bay area is easy. Freeways through Tracy and Oakdale zip you over to Sonora in three hours. Then it's a choice. Do you stay at old-time spots or inexpensive motels in town or head out of town to the Lazy Z Resort? Rental cabins, motels, and campgrounds up the hill a bit toward Pinecrest Lake and Strawberry add further choices.

Mi-wok Village is only three miles or so away with its tourist attractions, and it's only twenty miles east on Highway 108 to Pinecrest and Pinecrest Lake, its dandy and heavily stocked lake. Pinecrest serves up rental boats, riding, tennis, and anything else any summer tourist needs. Like Kennedy Meadows near the top of the Sonora Pass, it's a gateway to the Emigrant Wilderness Area with its dozens of lakes, miles of streams, and low, forgiving passes. Just stay off the main Sierra Crest trail to avoid the compulsive Mexico-to-Canada hikers.

In winter, visitors head twenty-five miles to Dodge Ridge Ski Area, a dandy family ski area that's one of the oldest and most traditional spots in the Sierra. Nearby Strawberry has a decent resort and is a good place to breakfast. As a rule, Highway 108 closes for the winter just past this point.

In spring and fall, lesser-known reservoirs, such as Beardsley on the Stanislaus River, offer boaters good trout fishing. The browns and rainbows in the Stanislaus, Clark's Fork, and Kennedy or Deadman's creeks lurk just a short walk from Highway 108 all the way to Sonora Pass. Kirman Lake, barely on the other side of the pass, has trophy brook trout. However, some of the best trout action in the Sierra—if you don't mind banks sometimes overgrown with blackberry bushes and keeping an eye out for rattlesnakes—lurks in the smaller tributary creeks that bottom most canyons within a twenty-mile radius of Twain Harte.

Hikers, horseback riders, snowmobilers, and cross-country skiers find trails for all seasons here. Some of the best summer trails head into the Sierras from pack stations at Kennedy Meadows and Pinecrest. While these trails get most of the winter and summer action, there are many more at lower elevations that deserve your time (except in summer when it's dry and dusty). There is some decent rafting and, downstream from Sonora, canoe water, as well as an interesting covered bridge and good bass angling.

If you just want to look, scenery improves as you follow Highway 108 up the hill. The Dardanelles and the open glades of Sugar Pine Country deserve a visit, and a host of campsites along Highway 108 or the Clark Fork make this possible.

Nearer Twain Harte, in the incredible tangle of winding two-lane roads that lace the Gold Country, you will find old mines, working cattle ranches, small b and bs, and much else that the typical tourist misses. So if you like a sense of exploration and are not thrilled by crowds, Twain Harte is the place to stay. Then, too, if you must have mobs, you can always visit Columbia or drive down the Big Oak Flat Road for a day's visit to Yosemite!

For more information:

Grass Valley Chamber of Commerce, 916-273-4667.

The Northern Sierras

84.

Sierra City—America's Smallest City?

Sierra City hides from tourists at the north end of Highway 49. For a spot that's less than an hour from Lake Tahoe or Reno, it doesn't get nearly as much action as it should. It does get rather more snow than the rest of the Highway 49 towns that cluster at about twenty-five hundred feet in elevation at the bottom edge of the snow line. It's nearly two thousand feet higher and, as a result, offers a longer spring, earlier fall, and cooler summer than the typical foothill community.

Restaurants, a store, and a handful of motels and inns offer convenient services just down the hill from Gold Lakes Basin. Of course, you can, if you like, stay in town, visit the small Sierra County Historical Museum a quarter mile east of town, or take a tour of the Kentucky Mine and Stamp Mill during summer.

Wiser folks chug on up the pass, turn north at Bassets Station onto Gold Lakes Road, and whomp up the hill to a dozen drive-in and hike-in lakes under the mass of the Sierra Buttes to the west. Lower Sardine Lake has a nifty resort with rental boats and three hearty meals a day. The road to Upper Sardine Lake offers rather better fishing and a challenge for 2WD vehicles.

If you want to swim on a hot day, try Sand Pond. Anglers do better at Packer Lake or either

Upper or Lower Salmon Lakes. Lower Salmon Lake and Packer Lake both have rustic lodges. The former rents cabins and such, and each includes a rowboat with three meals a day available. Salmon Lake Lodge has boats, a ferry, and biweekly barbecues.

Campers find Sand Pond's Lower Sardine campground worth a look, and there are a number of campgrounds without running water. It's first come, first served, so look before you leap.

However, the best part of Gold Lakes Basin hides behind the trail signs. The Pacific Crest Trail that runs from Mexico to Canada passes just west of road access, and laterals are particularly nice. So are the half dozen or so lakes within an hour's walk. Deer, Tamarack, Saxonia, and Volcano Lakes are all easy hikes for first-time backpackers.

Best of all, this area attracts more backpackers, tenters, and hikers than most. You can meet people around campfires and enjoy a Sierra experience that's sadly out of fashion in these RV days.

Do, if you like, push the summer season. May's wonderful and, if you don't mind sharing camps with hunters, September or even October offers accessible isolation.

To get there the fast way: Take Interstate 80 to Truckee, then go north on Highway 89 and west on Highway 49. Interstate 80 to Placerville and Highway 49 through Nevada City and Downieville offer superior scenery.

For more information:

USGS Topographical Map—Sierra City Quadrangle.

North Yuba Ranger Station, Star Route 1, Camptonville, CA 95922, 916-288-3231.

Salmon Lake Lodge, Sierra City, CA 96125, 415-771-0150.

Packer Lake Lodge, Sierra City, CA 96125, 916-862-1221.
Lower Sardine Lake, Box 216, Sierra City, CA 96125, 916-862-1196.

85.

Ski Donner Plus

In their haste to get to the better-known skiing areas, such as Squaw Valley, Alpine Meadows, Incline Village, or Northstar, California skiers pass up what many consider the best skiing in the Sierras. There's no argument about Royal Gorge Nordic Ski Resort. It's the biggest, probably the best, and certainly one of the most popular cross-country ski resorts in the world.

The four downhill areas here, Sugar Bowl, Boreal Ridge, Donner Ski Ranch, and Soda Springs, offer more specialized approaches. A Sierra Club Lodge, Soda Springs Lodge, an assortment of rental cabins, and modest services whip up a superior snow vacation.

Best of all, if you have to chain up to get to the pass, you don't remove chains in Truckee and then discover you must add them again down along the Truckee River on the way to Squaw Valley or Tahoe. Even better (unless you want to be snowed in), if weather closes in, you're on the home side of Donner Pass. And, best of all, Donner Pass almost always has more snow than other areas. Up to seventy feet of snow a season, and more than twenty on the ground let you start skiing early and continue until late in the year.

Royal Gorge Nordic Ski Resort: With more than a mile of double-set wide track and a skating track in the middle for each and every day of the year, Royal

Gorge Nordic Ski Resort's just about the best in the world. One set of tracks runs around Lake Van Norden. Another set starts at the big lodge in Serene Lakes and runs out to the ski-in lodge that's a wonderful spot for a few days or a week's vacation. Additional track systems sprawl out toward Devil's Peak, and you can even ski down to Rainbow Lodge, run by the same company, when conditions permit.

These multiple-track systems mean skiers with different ability and fitness levels can start and end at the same spot, or beginners can enjoy French onion soup at the ski-in lodge while the jocks charge on to Upper or Lower Cascade. This means that everyone has a great time.

Special equipment keeps tracks set daily. Ski schools are big enough so that classes divide up into narrow ability ranges for maximum progress. There are even tows for those who want to practice downhill or telemark techniques.

Sugar Bowl—Society Skiing: Sugar Bowl lets you go in by tram or drive to the new areas to control access. Its society image offers Austrian atmosphere and two wonderful mountains—one's named after Walt Disney and the other after Lincoln. Both mountains—Disney's our favorite—suit skiers who are intermediate and up. Both mountains offer north-facing slopes for long seasons and decent snow. Do, however, brown-bag as they've got you when you take the tram over the railroad tracks where restaurant and cafeteria prices are the usual ski outrage. Get there early: Parking is limited, and it can be a long walk.

Boreal Ridge—Hot Dogger's Delight: Boreal Ridge, the hot-dogger's heaven right on Interstate 80, suits those who like short steep runs and the teenage set who gang up here day and night. It's the easiest access area, and some drive up for the night skiing from Grass Valley or even Sacramento.

A batch of runs laces the steep, north-facing hill behind the lodge; there's more on the other side that backs up on Donner Ski Ranch. Runs are short, but you can get in a lot of vertical ones in a day. Beginners, and those not in late-season shape, find the short runs and short breaks make excellent sense and reduce injuries, too.

Donner Ski Ranch—All Round Affordable: Donner Ski Ranch pioneered snowboarding and offers 360-degree skiing off its upper lift from its wonderful site at the break of Old 40, the old Donner Pass Highway. The lowest prices around extend to the restaurant and to the wonderful season-end sales at the ski shop.

The 360-degree hill means you can always find perfect snow even in the spring. Just follow the melt around the hill and ski in good corn snow all day. The area's particularly well-suited to ski boarding and seems the most laid back of all pass resorts. The Ski Ranch best suits beginners to intermediates and is a hit with cross-country skiers too lame or lazy to herringbone up the hill on their own. Tip: The road to the peak lift is a fine cross-country or beginner's downhill, and there are decent intermediate runs off "the cliffs" and on the back side of the hill toward the Sierra Club Lodge.

Soda Springs Ski Hill—Family Fun: Soda Springs Ski Area, where you can keep track of the kids, suits family skiers. Three open runs face north, and decent, rarely crowded lifts let parents keep an eye on the small fry from the lodge deck. This keeps kamikaze kids off the expert slopes. There are some high intermediate spots, so this is a good choice if you have beginners in the group, and, like Boreal, short runs are a good warm-up area for first trips. There's also good snow for more advanced skiers.

Food and lift costs are low, and you can find the makings for dinner or affordable meals in the market and cafes next to the Soda Springs post office. I used to ski down the back of the runs to my house in Serene Lakes. So I'm a bit prejudiced.

Other Snow Stuff: There's a parking lot across Interstate 80 from Boreal near the tourism booth, where boondockers park before they ski up to Peter Grub Hut. Other cross-country trails run up to Lola Montez Lake north of the Soda Springs Fire Station. There's free skiing on a county road down through Royal Gorge and more casual tracks, trails, and snow play areas out of the Serene Lakes Lodge at the outlet of Serene Lakes. However, back-country cross-country skiers should have snow-survival skills—take a weekend seminar—and travel in groups.

Totally bonkers types might check on the infamous moonlight midnight ski run from the top of Donner Pass off Old 40 that ends, if you don't get caught in an avalanche or ski off a cliff, at the west end of Donner Lake.

More conservative visitors can check the Western Ski and Sport Museum at Boreal Ridge that's operated by the Auburn Ski Club—donations accepted. The Ridge also has biathlon, fifteen- and forty-meter ski-jump hills, and other training areas nearby.

For more information:

Royal Gorge Nordic Ski Resort, Box 1100, Soda Springs, CA 95728, 916-426-3871.

Sugar Bowl, Soda Springs, CA 95728, 916-426-3651.

Boreal Ridge Ski Area, Soda Springs, CA 95728, 916-426-3666.

Donner Ski Ranch, Soda Springs, CA 95728, 916-426-3635.
Soda Springs Ski Hill, Soda Springs, CA 95728, 916-426-3666.
Western Ski and Sports Museum, Soda Springs, CA 95728, 916-426-3313.

86.

Truckee and Its Reservoirs

Truckee is to Lake Tahoe as Atlanta Airport is to the South. No question but that Interstate 80 is the route to Tahoe, but there's a question when you watch four out of ten cars and RVs turn south toward Tahoe and the rest head down Interstate 80 for Reno. It's "What's north?" The answer is Boca, Stampede, and Prosser Reservoirs, the back route to Gold Lakes Basin and Sierra City, and a lateral route across the Sierras on dirt roads through Jackson Meadows Reservoir.

Truckee does deserve a look. Park if you can and check out Commercial Row and the downtown tourist strip. Peek at Jibboom and Spring Streets. If you'd like to learn to rock climb, check the shop on Spring. Then consider lunch or dinner. Just stay north of the railroad tracks so you don't get stuck behind one of the "too-many-cars-to-count" freights or dawdling Amtrak passenger trains.

While there's more selection in Tahoe City, prices seem lower here and in the grocery and chain stores west of town toward the Tahoe turnoff. Donner Party Memorial Park and Donner Lake are the last reasonably affordable spots where you can stock up on groceries if you camp or rent a cabin.

Donner Lake's a traditional Sierra destination as Highway 40, Old 40 for locals, crosses over a lovely arched bridge just east of the Sierra Crest that stopped the Donner Party. Then the road winds back down through some of the most popular climbing granite in the Sierras to the slender lake that's got surprisingly good fishing, wonderful sailing and sailboarding, and water cold enough to turn kids blue in short order.

At the east end of the lake, Donner Memorial Park shows what happens to the unprepared when early snows come in. Almost half the Donner Party perished; the rest lived out their lives with accusations of cannibalism. The Donner Memorial Monument in the park is the height of the twenty-two feet the snow supposedly packed to that year—that's not a record, and you get more snow up the hill in Soda Springs.

There's decent if usually crowded camping in the park, as well as the Emigrant Trail Museum's fair slide show and rather mediocre exhibits that may not be worth the modest admission cost. A number of lodges along the lake offer affordable lodgings, and there's golf at Tahoe-Donner and also toward Martis Reservoir.

Head out of Truckee onto Interstate 80 East and follow the Truckee River downstream to the turnoff to Boca and Stampede Reservoirs. Prosser Reservoir is a bit north on Highway 89 and a second choice for campers and everyone else except winter's ice anglers.

Do realize the Truckee River's one of the better brown-trout streams in California—check special regulations—and the Boca turnoff is both the route to the reservoirs and an access point to river fishing. A fishing guide's recommended.

Boca Dam is just a five-iron shot from Interstate 80, and the big impoundment seems better suited to sailing and personal watercraft than fishing. It's rather windy and Boca Rest Campground seems to

Donner Party Monument

suit the RV set better than tenters. Continue on up the Little Truckee—nice fishing where it swings away from the road—and you're at Stampede Reservoir with its scenic campgrounds, lovely views, and more decent fishing. You also can head out the other side of Stampede to connect to Highway 89. Stampede Reservoir is a fine camping choice for summers when the Tahoe basin fills, and the ramps work even in low-water years when the reservoir's drained fast to help water Reno.

If you stay on Highway 89 north out of

Truckee—stop at the ranger station and get a Tahoe National Forest Map—it's only fifteen miles or so to one of the best trans-Sierra routes, in past Jackson Meadows Reservoir where there's wonderful camping, good boating, and easy access to a couple of dozen local lakes. Some, such as Weaver, are private. Others, such as Faucherie, are incredibly beautiful and accessible only on dirt roads of dubious merit. One chain of lakes runs all the way across the Sierras, past Bowman Reservoir with its inlet camping areas, and on down to heavily stocked Fuller Lake with better camping in the PG&E (Pacific Gas & Electric) campground at the end of the paved road that continues down to Highway 20 some thirty miles east of Nevada City. With a 4WD, you can run back up to Highway 49.

From Bowman Reservoir, you also can rumble down to Washington (see Chapter 82, Progress and Preservation—Grass Valley and Nevada City) or dodge the trees and boulders over to Highway 49.

You also can turn downstream to the north just before you cross Jackson Meadows Dam and follow the river to tidy and scenic Milton Reservoir. Scramble anglers go with the river to wild trout down through a series of numbered box canyons. There's even a small wilderness area just south of Bowman Reservoir where, from the lateral road between Bowman and Fuller, you can drive to the lookout station at the top of the hill and hike downhill to a series of small lakes.

If you enjoy isolated campgrounds with decent fishing and limited crowds, this is the area to find it. Some sites, such as Fuller Lake, are run by the Pacific Gas & Electric Company; others are operated by Tahoe National Forest. Do bring a shovel, rope, and the skills needed to get unstuck—roads vary from year to year, and the local tow trucks charge a bundle when their trucks leave pavement!

For more information:

Pacific Gas & Electric Co., 800-552-4743.

Tahoe National Forest, Highway 49, Nevada City, CA 95959, 916-265-4531.

87.

Eagle Lake—Ospreys and Isolation

While Eagle Lake is best known for its huge trout and named after the national bird, you'll probably see more ospreys here than eagles. You will, if you work at it, catch some two-foot-long trout. For the angler, the best part of this is that you don't really need a boat. You can fish bait or cast flies from shore. But there's a lot more here than fishing that's usually blown away all summer anyhow. It's a good back door to Mount Lassen, the wonders of the lava beds, and the tidy back country around Silver Lake.

Since fishing traditionally opens here with a mob scene on Memorial Day weekend, wise visitors who like the open solitude should visit in the fall. Summer tends to blow you off the water—windsurfers take note! The campgrounds under the bluffs at the lake's south end do offer a protected spot to stay.

Winter's out as the marina and much else closes. It's cold in the fall, but you can fish from shore as cooling waters bring huge trout into casting range. Just head home if storms are forecast.

Spring also means birds, and you'll spot ospreys all year. Add seasonal waterfowl here, and at nearby Honey lake, and you've got a fine spot for birders who want to add Great Basin, arid buck brush, shore, and several ecological zones of Sierra and foothill birds to their life lists.

Hikers might want to mix in a visit to Silver Lake near Westwood on the Lassen National Forest. That's the easy access to the vest-pocket Caribou Wilderness handy for early- and late-season visits because it's at a modest five thousand- to seven-thousand-foot elevation without much in the way of climbs. There are at least eighteen small lakes, as well as volcanic delights left over from an 1800s and earlier eruptions. You can drive into and camp at Silver or nearby Caribou Lake. Supplies and lodgings can be found in Westwood on the way back to Interstate 5. Otherwise, the best way to get to Eagle Lake is up Highway 395 from Tahoe and Reno.

For more information:
Lassen National Forest, 916-257-2151.

88.

Spring or Fall for Tahoe

Lake Tahoe vacations offer a summer cooler that still attract mobs from the hot Central Valley. Add what many feel is the best collection of ski resorts in the world, and you know why locals adore spring and fall. Special off-season rates, a chance to get reservations at popular campgrounds such as Emerald Bay or Sugar Pine Point State Park, and seasonally uncrowded shops, restaurants, fishing, and hiking make California's favorite lake most attractive.

Of course, neither fall nor spring matches the "flatlander" calender. Fall starts after Labor Day weekend, but it ends when enough snow falls to lure skiers. Spring ends Memorial Day, but starts when the lifts close. So your window of opportunity can open wide or be nearly shut depending on the weather. A little snow to crunch under your feet won't hurt around the lake.

Realize that Tahoe travel, views, and fishing peak from dawn and dusk. Plan days to start as the sun rises, take a break or even a nap around noon, eat brunch or early dinner, and try to be at or near the lake as the stars come out. There's nothing more romantic.

Tip: The best way to see Tahoe is from a boat on the north end of the lake as the sun rises to paint the Sierras that hide Alpine Meadows and Squaw Valley. A good way to do this is to book a morning trip on a fishing boat. The view's worth the cost; lakers and the odd rainbow or brown seem a bonus. You also can book sternwheel trips out of South Tahoe that, in season, include dinner and dancing. There's another good view of the lake from South Tahoe casino restaurants, too.

Clearly food and lodgings run the full gamut. Camping suits any budget, and Tahoe offers a wide range of choices. The best campsites in California may be the boater's only sites on the north bank of Emerald Bay. These are reasonably convenient to South Tahoe for boaters. At the north end of the lake, Sugar Pine Point State Park—open all year—gets the nod. For more isolation you have a flock of good campsites along the Truckee River.

Other lodgings run from the posh casinos down to old-fashioned motels and b and bs. Casinos offer the best deals for lodging and food as gamblers pay for the overhead. Packages are particularly attractive. The Resort at Squaw Creek, an upscale spot in Squaw Valley, is at the high end. River Ranch, where summer raft trips end, is a good spot with a decent restaurant—try the duck.

The best restaurant at Tahoe may be Le Petit

Pier, an exceptional dinner house at the north end of the lake, but there are hundreds of options from Russian to ribs and more chain restaurants than most big cities. Casino buffets offer medium quality very, very inexpensively.

However, picnics seem ideally suited for Tahoe. Try Sand Harbor on the Nevada side or visit Sugar Pine Point where there's a lovely level hiking path. The bike paths that run from Tahoe City along the lake deserve a try on all but the coldest days.

It's a little silly to detail recreation at everyone's favorite lake. The problem is selecting the best activities. A short list might include a morning trail ride up out of Ponderosa on the Nevada side or the mile-long hike down to Vikingsholm on Emerald Bay—the hike back's another thing, so some visit the bay on tour boats out of South Tahoe.

For more information:

Tahoe-Donner Chamber of Commerce, 916-541-5255.

Index

Country
Roads Press
publishes books
that celebrate the spirit
and flavor of rural and small
town America. Far from strip malls
and chain stores, the heart of America
may still be found among the people
and places along its country
roads. We invite our
readers to travel
these roads
with us.